GHOSTHUNTING
MICHIGAN

AMERICA'S
HAUNTED ROAD TRIP

Titles in the *America's Haunted Road Trip* Series:

Ghosthunting Colorado
Ghosthunting Florida
Ghosthunting Kentucky
Ghosthunting Illinois
Ghosthunting Maryland
Ghosthunting Michigan
Ghosthunting New Jersey
Ghosthunting New York City
Ghosthunting North Carolina
Ghosthunting Ohio
Ghosthunting Ohio: On the Road Again
Ghosthunting Oregon
Ghosthunting Pennsylvania
Ghosthunting San Antonio, Austin, and Texas Hill Country
Ghosthunting Southern California
Ghosthunting Southern New England
Ghosthunting Texas
Ghosthunting Virginia

Chicago Haunted Handbook
Cincinnati Haunted Handbook
Nashville Haunted Handbook
Haunted Hoosier Trails
More Haunted Hoosier Trails
Spirits of New Orleans
Spooked in Seattle
Twin Cities Haunted Handbook

GHOSTHUNTING MICHIGAN

HELEN PATTSKYN

CLERISY PRESS

Ghosthunting Michigan

For further information, contact the publisher at:

Clerisy Press
An imprint of AdventureKEEN
306 Greenup Street
Covington, KY 41011
www.clerisypress.com

CATALOGING-IN-PUBLICATION DATA IS AVAILABLE FROM THE LIBRARY OF CONGRESS

ISBN 978-1-57860-513-2 (pbk.); ISBN 978-1-57860-514-9 (ebook);
ISBN 978-1-57860-591-0 (hardcover)

Distributed by Publishers Group West
Printed in the United States of America

Editor: Donna Poehner
Cover design: Scott McGrew
Cover and interior photos provided by the author unless otherwise noted

TABLE OF CONTENTS

Preface

DO YOU BELIEVE IN GHOSTS?

If you are like 52 percent of Americans (according to a recent Harris Poll), you *do* believe that ghosts walk among us. Perhaps you have heard your name called in a dark and empty house. It could be that you have awoken to the sound of footsteps outside your bedroom door, only to find no one there. It is possible that you saw your grandmother sitting in her favorite rocker chair, the same grandmother who had passed away several years before. Maybe you took a photo of a crumbling, deserted farmhouse and discovered strange mists and orbs in the photo, anomalies that were not visible to your naked eye.

If you have experienced similar paranormal events, then you know that ghosts exist. Even if you have not yet experienced these things, you are curious about the paranormal world, the spirit realm. If you weren't, you would not now be reading this preface.

Over the last several years, I have investigated haunted locations across the country, and with each new site, I found myself becoming more fascinated with ghosts. What are they? How do they manifest themselves? Why are they here? These are just a few of the questions I have been asking. No doubt, you have been asking the same questions.

The books in the *America's Haunted Roadtrip* series can help you find the answers to your questions about ghosts. We've gathered together some of America's top ghost writers (no pun intended) and researchers and asked them to write about their states' favorite haunts. Each location that they write about is open to the public so that you can visit them for yourself and try out your ghosthunting skills. In addition to telling you about their often hair-raising adventures, the writers have included maps and travel directions so that you can take your own haunted roadtrip.

People may think that Michigan is all about lakes and woods, hunting and fishing, cherry orchards and Motor City, but Helen Pattskyn's *Ghosthunting Michigan* proves that the Great Lakes State is fertile ground for entities even more fantastic than the 1960 Edsel Ranger. This book is a spine-tingling trip through Michigan's small towns and lively cities, its historic sites and fun spots, all of them haunted. Ride shotgun with Helen as she seeks out ghosts of seamen—the crew of the *Edmund Fitzgerald*—at the Whitefish Point Lighthouse and Shipwreck Museum and the spirits of thespians who took their final bows long ago at the Baldwin Theatre in Royal Oak. Travel with her to Camp Ticonderoga where a top-hatted phantom sits at a table, waiting for service. If you're lucky—or, perhaps, unlucky—you might run into the ghost of jilted Minnie Quay at Forester Pier, on Lake Huron's shore. And who was that ghostly woman who walked right through a door at Bone Head's BBQ in Willis? Hang on tight; *Ghosthunting Michigan* is a scary ride.

But once you've finished reading this book, don't unbuckle your seatbelt. There are still 49 states left for your haunted roadtrip! See you on the road!

John Kachuba
Editor, *America's Haunted Roadtrip*

Southeastern Michigan

Brownstown
  Marlow's Chill & Grill

Detroit
  The Whitney

Fenton
  Fenton Hotel Tavern & Grille

Holly
  Battle Alley Arcade Antiques Mall
  Holly Hotel
  Main Street Antiques

Royal Oak
  Baldwin Theatre

Troy
  Camp Ticonderoga

Willis
  Bone Head's BBQ

CHAPTER 1

The Whitney

DETROIT

WHEN PEOPLE THINK ABOUT DETROIT, they often think of sports: the Tigers, the Red Wings, the Lions, and the Pistons. Or they think about the auto industry, because Detroit is still "Motor City." It's also the home of Motown Records, where so many rock and roll greats got their start. Other people think of Detroit and remember the riots in the 1960s, or think about the crime rate, the problems with the school system, and all the rundown neighborhoods. When I think of Detroit, I think of shopping at Eastern Market for fresh produce—my husband is convinced that we have to arrive by 5 a.m., or "all the good stuff will be gone." I always tell him I'll take my chances, we don't *really* need to get there before 8 a.m. Eastern Market is only open on Saturday, and Saturdays are for sleeping in. My other favorite places in the city are the Detroit Public Library, the Detroit Institute of Art, the Opera House, Symphony Hall, the Fox Theatre, and, of course, the Whitney restaurant.

Located on Woodward Avenue, just a few blocks from the campus of Wayne State University and Detroit's cultural center, the Whitney was once one of the city's oldest and most beautiful private residences. Now it is one of the city's finest and most beautiful restaurants. I've only been there to eat on a couple of very special occasions, but I fell immediately in love with the grand old house. Of course, prior to my visit on a bright sunny afternoon in April, I had only gone in looking for after-theater drinks and desert with friends, not hoping for a glimpse of the ghost of former owner, David Whitney Jr.

Construction on the 52-room, Romanesque-style home began in 1890 and was completed four years later. One local newspaper described the house as "the most elaborate and substantial residence in this part of the country." The exterior walls of the mansion are made of South Dakota jasper, a rare type of pink granite. Inside, the first things visitors see are the immense staircase in the Grand Hall, with its beautiful Tiffany stained glass panels, and a huge, ornate fireplace. There are 19 other fireplaces throughout the house, a secret vault hidden in the original dining room, and an elevator. A *haunted* elevator, according to stories. But ghosts aside, the Whitney mansion was one of the first homes of its day to boast such a modern convenience.

David Whitney Jr. was born in 1830 and came to Detroit at the age of 27, in 1857; he died in 1900, but his family continued to live in the house until the 1920s, when it was sold and became the home of the Wayne County Medical Society, which in turn later sold it to the Visiting Nurses Association some years later. In 1980, Richard Kughn purchased the property, and after six years of restoration, the Whitney opened

up as "an American restaurant in an American palace." Kughn
sold the property in 2007 to Bud Liebler, who continues to carry
on the tradition of excellence started by his predecessor. In addition to the beautiful dining rooms on the main floor, there are
outdoor garden parties all summer long, and the Ghost Bar up
on the third floor.

When I spoke to David, one of the many wonderful staff
members, I asked him if he had ever had any unusual experiences while working there—or if maybe any of his coworkers
had seen or heard anything out of the ordinary.

"We have a lot of the usual stuff, I guess," he told me. "Doors
sometimes shut as if by themselves. And one woman who used
to work here told me that she was walking through the Great
Hall, and one of the crystals, from one of the chandeliers, fell
right at her feet and shattered. It kind of freaked her out a bit.
Of course that might not have had anything to do with anything
supernatural," he cautioned. "And if you knew her . . . she's a bit
of a spirit herself," he added with a chuckle.

Ah, yes, I've known people like that, too.

David went on to tell me that the Highland Ghost Hunters
had been in a couple of times and spent the night, investigating the building. "They said that they heard piano playing late
at night, after all the staff had gone home. I think that would
have been Grace Whitney. Grace was David Whitney's favorite
daughter and quite an accomplished musician," he explained.
"She played several instruments, and, in fact, the Whitneys
used to open up the house and hold recitals so people could
come and listen to her playing. Anyway, Grace was overseas
when her father took ill. Of course back then, you couldn't just
hop on a plane and come home, so by the time she got here,
he'd already died. The Ghost Hunters said they also picked up a
male voice that same night, saying *I'm still here*. That was probably David Whitney."

The "infamous" second-floor elevator door at the Whitney.

Of course, one of the most haunted places in the building is said to be the elevator, especially where it opens up onto the second floor. Not only did David Whitney Jr. pass away in the house, his wife, Sara, also died there. Numerous employees have reported that the elevator will start moving on its own and that the doors open and close without anyone pushing the button.

I asked if it would be all right to have a look around and take some photographs—although there are several public areas up on both the second and third floors, I like to ask permission, especially before taking pictures. I was welcomed to take as many photos as I liked and to go anywhere that wasn't marked "private." Of course, I would behave myself, I always do—but what I wouldn't have given for a tour of the *whole* house.

I wandered up to the second floor and took a couple of photos of the elevator before exploring every open-to-the-public room, just because I love old architecture and antiques. Finally, I meandered up the stairs to the third floor and the aptly named Ghost

The foyer of the Whitney.

Bar. The bar wasn't open yet, but the bartender was setting up. He gave me a friendly "hello" and asked how I was doing.

"I'm doing great, thanks," I answered. Then I told him that I was writing a book about haunted places and that, naturally, the Whitney had come up.

The bartender smiled. "As long as you remember that everything I tell you is hearsay—that nothing's official—I've got a couple of stories for you, if you have a second and are interested."

"Absolutely." I was very interested and I had somehow managed to find unmetered parking on a nearby side street, so I had all afternoon!

"I've been a bartender here for about a year," he began, "and customers are always asking me if I've ever seen anything weird—you know, anything 'ghostly.' I haven't. But I've had some customers who said they did."

He told me that the first incident had occurred during a wedding in which the entire mansion had been rented out. "The way they run it is pre-dinner drinks are up here, then they serve dinner downstairs, and then we reopen the bar for post-dinner drinks," he told me. "There weren't very many children at this wedding, but there was this one little girl. She was maybe five or six and she kept running around and she didn't want to sit still. Her mom asked me if I'd mind keeping an eye on her for a few minutes, so she could go down and get something to eat. Everyone else had gone downstairs by then, and I really didn't mind, so I said 'sure,' and let the mom go downstairs. I left the little girl alone in this room, and I went into that room over there," he pointed to one of the sitting rooms adjacent to the bar.

"I was in there cleaning up, and all of the sudden, I heard this shriek, so I came running out to see what had happened. The little girl had this look on her face, like she was totally terrified. I didn't see anyone—or anything—so I asked her what was wrong. She told me that a big ball of light had flown out of one corner of the room and came right at her. And she was really frightened," he emphasized. "This was before the 'Ghost Bar' sign was up, and she was way too young to know the history of the place—and way too young to make up something like that. She was okay after that, but I've never seen a little kid so scared."

The bartender went on to tell me about another incident that happened about a month after that wedding reception, this time with a little boy who came upstairs with his mother. "He was right about the same age, too, I think. I didn't pay too much attention to them; they were just looking around. Then all of the sudden, I see this little boy dart out of that room and into the other room. I probably still wouldn't have thought too much of it, except I overheard him telling his mother, 'Mommy, Mommy, there it goes!' A few seconds later the mother came over to me and said that she was so sorry, but her son kept insisting he was being chased around by a ball of light."

The third incident involved an adult, a guy who had been sitting at the bar having a drink. "He was about my age," said the bartender, which would probably have made his customer somewhere in his mid-20s. "And he was talking on his cell phone, making plans to meet up with his buddies somewhere downtown. I turned away to take care of another customer. The next thing I knew this guy had jumped up out of his seat and was standing way over there, looking really freaked out. I asked him if he was okay, and he insisted that, yeah, he was fine. 'Are you sure?' I asked a second time. He looked pretty shaken up and I thought— I don't know, maybe he'd seen a mouse or something. This is an old building. 'No, I'm good, bro,' he told me. But he didn't sit back down. Instead, he told me he was ready to cash out."

The bartender said that as his customer was settling up his tab, he'd finally calmed down enough to admit that he'd seen the silhouette of a man standing behind him in the mirror behind the bar—but when he turned around, nobody was there.

Before I left, he took me over to one of the two side rooms— the one opposite the bar—and told me that that room was the one where people have complained about feeling "negative energy."

"Especially women," he told me. "Ladies come up here and they're just not comfortable in this room."

We talked for a few more minutes about paranormal phenomena in general, and I took a few more photographs before leaving the mansion.

Just a few blocks down from the Whitney is the Majestic Theatre, which is more than just a theater, I discovered when I popped in for a quick visit. I found both a café and a bowling alley—sadly, I didn't find any credible ghost stories. Still, the stage of the Majestic Theatre is the last place where Harry Houdini played before he died, and it's well worth checking out if you're in the area.

Marlow's Chill & Grill
BROWNSTOWN

WHEN YOU MENTION THE DOWNRIVER AREA, most Detroiters think of the Gibraltar Trade Center, Flat Rock Speedway, Trenton Scarecrow Festival, or Cruisin' Downriver, an antique car event that rivals the northern suburb's Woodward Dream Cruise. Crusin' Downriver, which draws thousands of spectators each summer, stretches through Lincoln Park, Wyandotte, Southgate, and Riverview.

Most people don't think about ghosts when you mention the downriver area, especially if you happen to be talking about the township of Brownstown. But that's exactly where I ended up one Monday afternoon in late November, on the trail of a promising lead I found on the Motor City Ghost Hunters' website. I took my husband along for the ride, telling him it would make for a fun date. We hadn't been out to eat in a while, and even though a sports bar wouldn't normally be our first choice for a date night, we both love a good burger. He was a little dubious at first, not because he knew I was going on another one of my "ghosthunting adventures," but because, unlike me, he is simply not a very adventurous soul. The idea of a 45-minute trek downriver for a burger wasn't exactly the highlight of his day. He came anyway.

Marlow's is located on a rural stretch of Telegraph Road, just a short way down from the Oak Ridge Cemetery, which rumor has it is also haunted. According to an urban legend, the ghosts of a little boy and a tall man can be spotted in the cemetery between the hours of 9 p.m. and 3 a.m.—however, it is worth noting that like most cemeteries, Oak Ridge is closed after dark, and trespassers will be prosecuted. Visiting the cemetery during the day is perfectly legal, of course.

Other specters are said to roam the streets of the nearly 200-year-old town. Rumors abound of "strange apparitions" that supposedly wander the streets of the Tele Valley mobile home park and of a "ghostly man" who has allegedly been seen roaming the woods in Dawnshire Park near the Civic Center. Again, I don't recommend visiting either location after dark, but it's perfectly legal to walk around the Civic Center during the day. Just remember, you can't believe everything you read on the Internet, especially when it comes to ghostly hauntings. I learned that when I visited Calumet and Eagle Harbor earlier in the year.

It was early evening when my husband and I arrived in Brownstown. We found ourselves before a large, beige brick-and-wood paneled building bearing a sign that read MARLOW'S CHILL & GRILL. I have to admit, I wasn't expecting the drive to be worth it; Marlow's does not *look* like a hundred-year-old haunted tavern, even if it does have a rather colorful history. The building has served many functions, under many different owners, over the last century. In addition to being the home of numerous pubs and taverns, the building at one time housed a brothel in the upstairs apartment, and at another point in history, it served as a station house for the Brownstown mounted police. When we got there, the parking lot was mostly empty. For a moment I wondered if the place was open. As usual, I hadn't called ahead.

We parked anyway and headed up to the door to discover that yes, they were open, just not very busy yet. (At this point, my husband really wanted to know what I'd dragged him into!) Inside, Marlow's was everything you would expect from a friendly blue-collar neighborhood sports bar. Several televisions hung over the bar, sports memorabilia dotted the walls, and there was even a dance floor. In addition to bar seating, we found booths along one wall and had a seat. We didn't have long to wait before a friendly server came over to greet us with a smile and a couple of menus. Our server's name was Ashley. As we were talking, I learned that she had worked at Marlow's for awhile. But before asking about the bar's resident specters, I decided what I really wanted was dinner. Ashley took our orders and put them into the kitchen. When she returned to check on us, I told her the real reason for my visit.

"This place is totally freaky!" she exclaimed. It took no prompting at all to get Ashley to tell me about some of the things she and other staff members had experienced at the bar. "We think one of the ghosts is a waitress who was murdered at the bar. The story I heard was that it was a customer who killed her. She was sitting on one of the bar stools, and he came up behind her and slit her throat."

No one has ever been able to dig up enough hard evidence to prove that someone was really murdered on the property, but it seems to be a widely held belief. Ashley told me that sometimes glasses fall off the shelves for no apparent reason, usually by the ice maker. "One night, I was standing right there," she went on, pointing over to the bar. "I think I'd been here for a couple of months, so I guess it was maybe last August. Anyway, I swear, I felt someone touching my face, like this," she demonstrated, sliding one finger down the side of her face, from her hairline all the way to her chin. "It freaked me right out."

Marlow's other resident specter is a much more negative entity, according to paranormal investigators and bar staff alike. He can be felt most strongly around the ladies' restroom and in the upstairs apartment, which is no longer used for anything except storage. Ashley said that most of the staff avoids the apartment and hardly anyone will go up there alone. "*No one* would live there," she added.

"One night, after closing," she continued, "the night bartender literally came *running* out of the bathroom, screaming. She said she'd been in the stall and felt somebody running their fingers through her hair, like they were standing behind her."

Okay, that would be enough to shake me up, too, and I don't rattle that easily. Ashley told me that a number of staff members and even some customers have felt as if they were being watched in and around the restrooms (even when there was no one else around), and a few have also reported being touched, although the night bartender's experience was by far the most extreme. Most of what the staff experiences seems to happen when they're cleaning up, after closing.

But what I wanted to know more about was the apartment upstairs. Being the brave soul that I am, I asked if it would be all right to go up and take pictures. Ashley said she didn't think it would be a problem, but she put in a call to the owner, Robert Marlow, just to double-check.

About then, our food was ready, so while Ashley called her boss, I scribbled down a few notes and my husband dug into his burger. "Well?" I asked him.

He wasn't sure if I was asking about the burger or the ghosts, so he just shrugged. As far as *I* was concerned, the ghost stories were more than worth the drive downriver. (But I enjoyed my dinner too.)

When Ashley returned, she let me know that Marlow didn't mind me going upstairs. The only catch was that nobody had a key, so would I mind coming back tomorrow? Not at all!

While I munched on my fries, Ashley told us about the Motor City Ghost Hunters' visit in 2010. "They were here most of the night with all their equipment. They're the ones who told us that there were two different spirits, the woman at the bar and the other one upstairs. They got a bunch of stuff on tape." If you visit the Motor City Ghost Hunters website, you can see for yourself the picture of an orb that they caught downstairs in the bar area and hear clips of the EVP (electronic voice phenomena) that was recorded during their visit.

By then other customers were drifting in, so Ashley left me and my husband to finish our food. I did visit the ladies' room before we left, but, alas, if the ghost was about, he wasn't in the mood to play with any customers that night.

I returned the next afternoon and was shown around back by the bar's manager. He unlocked the door to the upstairs storage area, flipped on the light, and with hardly a word, retreated hastily back into the bar. Maybe he was too busy to accompany me upstairs, but I had to admit it was a little odd, being left to wander around on my own like that, even though Ashley was right about there not being much upstairs. The upper floor of Marlow's was clearly hardly used at all. I took a number of photographs and left my digital recorder switched on, hoping I might see or hear something interesting. No such luck. I didn't feel especially uneasy, either. Maybe I'll have better luck somewhere else.

Before I left, I made sure to lock up, and I thanked Ashley again for all her help and promised her that the next time I'm downriver, I'll stop back by for a burger . . . and maybe take another shot at ghosthunting!

Camp Ticonderoga
TROY

I FIRST DISCOVERED CAMP TICONDEROGA a decade or so ago. At the time, I was waiting tables at a little Coney Island restaurant in Royal Oak, and, like most waitresses, I kept tabs on my regular customers—their names, their usual order, where they worked, etc. That's how I met S. (I haven't seen him in years, so I couldn't ask him if it was all right to use his name.) It was pretty obvious what S. did for a living the first time he came in wearing a chef's coat and checked pants, so I asked him where he worked.

"Camp Ticonderoga," he told me.

"I have friends who eat there all the time. They told me it's haunted."

I hadn't actually taken my friends seriously, but S. looked me dead in the eye and said, "Yeah, that's Hannah. Everybody at Camp Ti knows her."

I didn't believe S. any more than I believed my friends. "Come on, you *really* expect me to believe your workplace is haunted?" Surely, S. and his coworkers were mistaking the sounds of an old building settling for the sounds of ghosts. But S. assured me that he didn't believe in ghosts either before he started working there.

It didn't take long before he changed his mind, however. "Lights flicker on and off all the time, and I swear the elevator has a mind of its own," he told me. "The elevator door opens and shuts when no one is even near it, let alone in it. Sometimes other doors slam shut, and dishes fall off the shelves in the kitchen," he added.

Needless to say, I was intrigued, so I decided to check it out—besides, the food was supposed to be pretty good, so at worst, I'd be disappointed in the ghost but get a good meal.

On my next day off, I drove up Rochester Road and arrived at the sprawling old farmhouse-turned-restaurant a little before the dinner rush. As soon as I was settled at a table, I asked my waitress if the place was really haunted. "Oh, yes, absolutely." She told me the same things my friend the chef had, adding that Hannah had lived in the house around the turn of the century. The story was that she hanged herself from the rafters in one of the bedrooms—that area is now a part of the upstairs dining room. I was glad I was on the main floor.

"Why did she kill herself?" I asked.

"I don't think anyone knows."

I didn't think much about Camp Ti or Hannah again until I started writing about Michigan's haunted places and decided that it was past time to revisit the restaurant.

The building was originally a farmhouse that belonged to

Elizabeth and Henry Blount and was built in the early 1820s, just after the city of Troy was settled. Elizabeth and Henry raised seven children in the large two-story home and eventually passed the property down to their grandsons, Harry and Frank. The Blount family continued to live in the home until May 13, 1924, when the farm was sold and ultimately developed into the Sylvan Glen Golf Course. The developers turned the old farmhouse into a restaurant. It has had many different names over the decades, including the Double Eagle, the Wooden Horse, and the Shark Creek Inn. In 1996, it became Camp Ticonderoga—or Camp Ti, for short.

According to their website, the restaurant is "an upscale, yet rustic, bar and grill . . . Camp Ti boasts a comfortable, inviting Adirondack atmosphere. . . ." That description doesn't really do justice to the rugged log-cabin interior with its three huge stone fireplaces, antler chandeliers, and mounted hunting trophies on the walls. My favorite part of the décor is right inside the door, where you'll find Camp Ti's "dog wall." The owners are self-avowed "dog people" and love to have their customers bring in pictures of their canine companions. Once a month a "mutt of the month" is chosen and the lucky dog gets a doggy bag filled with goodies from the kitchen.

For its human clientele, Camp Ti serves up a variety of menu options, ranging from salads and homemade soups to Black Angus steak and specials such as traditional shepherd's pie, "buffaloaf" (buffalo meatloaf), and venison stew. Throughout the year, Camp Ti hosts a number of themed parties, including its annual "beach bash" in March. Guests are encouraged to wear their favorite Hawaiian shirt and play on an artificial beach. Anyone who lives in Michigan knows that by March, we're ready for a little "sun and sand," even if we have to create it ourselves.

I could have used some sun and sand myself, on the cold, snowy winter day I chose to return to Camp Ticonderoga, on my hunt for more stories about Hannah. I went in for lunch and got a quiet table overlooking the golf course. And it was just my luck—I got the *one* waitress who was even more skeptical than I am about the paranormal. I told her about the book I was writing and asked her about Hannah. Her response was an almost apologetic confession: "I don't believe in ghosts."

I asked her if she would mind explaining why she felt that way. "I'm not out to prove or disprove anything," I promised. "I'm just gathering peoples' stories. It might make a good balance to hear from someone who doesn't believe this place is haunted."

"It's an old building," my waitress reminded me. "So if the lights flicker I figure it's just the wiring. The elevators are old too, so if the doors open and shut unexpectedly, it's just a mechanical thing. I've never felt creeped out anywhere in the restaurant. People are always making something out of nothing, you know?"

Fair enough, but I still hoped to talk to someone about Hannah—after all, I had already met several people who were convinced she still haunted Camp Ti. My server was happy to help out by introducing me to the manager on duty. The restaurant was starting to get a little busy by then, so I exchanged business cards with the manager and arranged to come back another time. I was put in touch with assistant manager, Christy Hardy, who, I was told, had been at Camp Ti for about ten years and was something of an expert when it came to Hannah. She had also had a few personal experiences with Hannah—and apparently some other ghosts as well.

Christy met me the following Sunday afternoon—she was very sweet and quite happy to give me a few minutes of her time. After getting us each a glass of soda, she settled us at a quiet table near the second bar, toward the back of the restaurant so we could talk. I explained my book and asked her what she could tell me about Camp Ticonderoga's ghosts.

"When I first started here, I remember walking up the stairs to the second floor and seeing a man sitting at a table, near the staircase. I thought it was a little odd, as no one was supposed to be up there; that part of the dining room was closed. He was dressed kind of funny too, in a vintage suit, like something you'd have seen a hundred years ago, and he was wearing a top hat. And then suddenly, he was gone." She explained that she was a little freaked out, but then another manager said she had seen the same man sitting there on a different occasion. "We had another manager quit, after just a couple of days," she added. "I don't know why, but . . ." she shrugged, leaving it open-ended.

The man in the top hat wasn't the only ghost the staff has reported seeing—or experiencing in other ways.

Christy told me about a server who had napkin-wrapped silverware roll right off the table upstairs. "She didn't think too much of it at first, she just picked it up and put a clean roll in its place. That rolled off the table too. It happened twice more, really freaking her out. There are several people who won't go upstairs by themselves."

Christy went on, "Some people claim to have been touched, but when they turn to see who's there, there isn't anyone nearby. And a lot of people have experienced cold spots upstairs. It's like you'll be walking along and suddenly get freezing cold for no reason." She also said that several people, both guests and staff, have reported hearing footsteps on the staircase leading up to the second floor. "But when they turn around, there's no one there. People hear children's voices too. And we have a ghost cat," she added, telling me how numerous people have reported hearing it meowing, especially when there aren't many customers around and the restaurant is quiet.

"One day I heard it and I was so sure it was a real cat that had gotten stuck up in the attic, I asked one of the cooks to go check it out. When he came down, he said that there was no cat.

There wasn't any evidence that any kind of animal had gotten in recently, either."

I had to admit, it seemed like there was an awful lot of seemingly supernatural activity at Camp Ticonderoga. It was little wonder the place had been investigated by so many paranormal investigators.

Christy explained to me that she's not really afraid of the ghosts, but sometimes locking up alone at night is a little nerve-wracking. She said she preferred to turn the lights off in the back first and then make her way toward the front door, so that the last lights to go off are the ones nearest the doors. She also repeated the story I'd heard before about how sometimes doors around the restaurant seem to open and shut by themselves. "One night it happened to me after closing, and I kept calling 'who's there?' but no one answered. No one was here."

There was another night, Christy told me, when she locked up and headed toward her car in the parking lot. She chanced to turn around and glance back at the building and swore that she saw a pair of blue glowing eyes watching her in the window. "Those windows there, behind the bar," she told me, pointing to the windows behind the main bar area. She didn't go back in to investigate. I wasn't sure I blamed her; I doubt I would have gone back in, either.

CHAPTER 4

Baldwin Theatre
ROYAL OAK

LIVING PRACTICALLY WITHIN WALKING distance of the Baldwin Theatre, I decided to take a chance and dropped in unannounced, even though it was close to Christmas. I knew there was a good chance I might not get to actually talk to anyone that day—but it was a good excuse to walk around downtown Royal Oak and get some last-minute shopping done.

I arrived at the Baldwin during regular box office hours and was greeted by Vonnie Miller. As soon as I explained the reason for my visit, she invited me into the office to talk. Unfortunately, she was the only person in just then and couldn't actually show me around, but Vonnie confirmed that the theater was "very haunted." She added that the Baldwin has been in a couple of books and has hosted several "haunted" events, where the audience is presented with the theater's history, along with its ghost stories.

I'd already read several newspaper articles about the Baldwin's ghosts and knew that the theater was a favorite stop on Halloween "ghost tours," as well as a favorite stop for paranormal investigators. There have been numerous pictures of orbs taken on both stages, as well as EVP (electronic voice phenomena) recordings of strange voices, and reports of sharp drops in temperature throughout the theater. It seems that when ghosts are around, the ambient temperature drops significantly. These so-called "cold spots" are a good indication of paranormal activity—after you've ruled out all of the logical explanations, like open doors or drafty windows.

Vonnie told me whom I really needed to talk to was Development Director Lesley Branden-Phillips. Lesley was off for the Christmas holiday, but Vonnie gave me her card and suggested I call the following week to set up an appointment.

I took advantage of the bright, mild afternoon to get some shots of the exterior of the building before heading off to do some Christmas shopping. Royal Oak is a hub for the arts community in Oakland County and has been one of my favorite places to visit since I was a teenager. Summer is my favorite time to be there, when the streets are crowded with pedestrians, making it a great time to people-watch. No matter what time of year it is, though, there's always something fun and interesting happening in Royal Oak.

In March, classical-music lovers can enjoy the Baroque Music Festival, while cinema buffs can travel a couple of miles up Woodward Avenue to enjoy the Uptown Film Festival. April brings Royal Oak's annual Earth Day/Green Living festival to the Detroit Zoo (which is actually located in the city of Royal Oak). June is marked by an annual fine-art fair, but the big arts event is in late August, when more than 200 musical acts fill up ten stages on Royal Oak's streets for the Arts, Beats, and Eats festival. For more great food, visit in November for the Annual Royal Oak Chili Cook Off, where professional chefs and amateurs alike compete for the title of the best chili in town. One of these years, I'm going to convince my husband to enter.

Even when there isn't a fair or festival going on, Royal Oak's shopping district—about a mile-long stretch down the city's two main roads, Washington and Main Street—is filled with dozens of specialty boutiques, art galleries, vintage-clothing stores, and an amazing variety of restaurants, pubs, and coffee shops. And in the heart of it all is the Baldwin Theatre, home of the Stagecrafters community theater company. The Stagecrafters originally called the nearby city of Clawson their home. They began there in 1956, when Clawson residents Robert Johnson, then a sophomore at Michigan State University, and Sally Bosz, a senior at Clawson High School, decided to start a summer theater program. With a cast and crew of only 30 people, the company—then known as the Clawson Community Club Players—performed Noel Coward's *Blithe Spirit* as a part of Clawson's annual Fourth of July celebration. The play was performed in the Clawson Elementary gymnasium and was declared "a hit" by local newspapers.

Because of the success of their first production, the company decided it needed to move to a bigger venue and was granted the use of the auditorium at Madison Height's John Page Middle School. With the move to a new city, the troupe decided to change its name, and in 1957 the Stagecrafters company was officially born.

Over the next decade the troupe grew and eventually returned to Clawson, where they purchased an old church on Bowers Street. The first play to debut at the Bowers Street Playhouse was Joseph Kesselring's *Arsenic and Old Lace*; the year was 1971.

The Main Stage auditorium of the Baldwin Theatre.

The company continued to grow, and in 1983 the Stagecrafters were invited by the International Amateur Theatre Association to take part in an exchange program with a theater troupe in England. They visited St. Albans the following year to perform on the stage of the Abbey Theatre.

By the following year, they knew it was time to move again; they needed a bigger theater with more space for rehearsals, a larger stage, and more room for building sets. When the city of Royal Oak offered them the Baldwin Theatre, the company took up a collection for the down payment, took out a mortgage to cover the rest, and purchased the property. They renamed their theater "The Baldwin." The article on the Baldwin's home page describes the restoration on the old, long-abandoned building as both a "Herculean task" and a "labor of love"—after talking to Lesley it was easy to see that that wasn't an exaggeration.

After Christmas, I called and set up an appointment to come back to the theater. Lesley met me at the box-office door and walked me through the back halls to the lobby, and then onto the main stage. She told me that the Baldwin was originally a silent-movie house and that it was older than the more well-known Fox Theatre, in downtown Detroit. Also, that when it was first built, back in 1922, "the Baldwin was considered the grandest theater in the Midwest." Looking out at the auditorium from the main stage, I had no difficulty believing that.

"All of this has been restored," Lesley said, as I was admiring the architectural décor, much of it reminiscent of Greek murals. "All of the murals you're looking at were covered up by truly awful-looking yellow curtains—we had *no* idea what we would find behind them. It was a pleasant surprise, but it was a lot of work to make this place beautiful again." The walls, Lesley told me, had been painted in what could only be described as a hideous shade of "blood red."

"The auditorium originally seated 1,400 guests, but we knew a community theater would never need that much seating, so we created the lobby area at the back and turned the mezzanine into our lighting and tech booth."

Lesley also told me that the Baldwin's pipe organ—once a staple in silent-movie houses—was still operational and that they host a couple of pipe organ concerts each year. "We have one of the few functioning pipe organs in the state," she added. As she continued with the theater's history, I learned that after the silent-movie era, the Baldwin hosted vaudeville performances. "Rumor has it Houdini performed here," said Lesley, "but it's *just* a rumor." In the 1950s, the Baldwin was converted over to "talkies"—talking pictures—and first-run movies were shown. But by the 1960s, the theater began its long, slow decline, showing only second-run films. The theater finally shut down after a fire in 1984. It was shortly thereafter that the city of Royal Oak sold the theater to the Stagecrafters, and they began their long and loving restoration process.

In addition to the main stage on the first floor, there is a second, smaller stage built into the old balcony area, behind the lighting/tech booth, where smaller productions are shown.

Lesley told me that she's had a number of paranormal investigators come through and has heard lots of stories from employees and patrons alike about ghosts. She invited me to follow her backstage and explained that quite a few people have claimed to hear "deliberate, slow" footsteps in the wings, just under the rigging, even though no one else was anywhere nearby. Next she led the way downstairs to the "green room," where actors hang out between scenes. It's also where the Stagecrafters's costumers work, creating wardrobes for each of the company's productions—as many as ten plays per year on both stages and as a part of their youth program.

"What most people don't know is that this used to be a fallout shelter," Lesley added, as we walked down the narrow stairs. It's also where there has been the most spectral activity in the past. "People have said they felt like they were being watched. I've even had people say they felt like someone had touched them down here," said Lesley.

She pointed out the door to the orchestra pit and said that when she first came to the theater, no one seemed to be able to photograph it clearly. Pictures were always distorted or clouded over; many had orbs in them. "It's been quiet the last couple of years," she added, explaining that in the beginning she had so many people coming through that she wonders if maybe the ghosts got annoyed and went away—or at least have decided to lie low for a while. "You're the first person I've had through here in almost a year." I felt both flattered and grateful to Lesley for giving me not only so much of her time, but also allowing me to tour the theater and write about it.

She went on to tell me about one particular incident in which a theater worker—he's not with the theater any longer, although that has nothing to do with the ghosts—came downstairs to find that all of the furniture and a bunch of boxes that he'd stacked up earlier in the day had all been moved to the center of the room. At first, he assumed the actors or staff members were pulling a prank, but everyone who was there denied having anything to do with it. Not only was the man in question one of the most honest people Lesley said she'd ever worked with, but also he didn't see any reason to doubt his colleagues—and there hadn't been very many people around that day, anyway.

Lesley led the way through a labyrinth of corridors to the wig and makeup rooms, back up the stairs to the lobby and up to the second stage. "We've probably had as much activity up here as down in the green room," she told me, although the second stage has also been quiet the last few years.

Lesley told me about one man's particularly harrowing experience in the second stage area. Behind the stage is the lighting/tech booth, for the lower, main stage. One of the stagehands was going about his business when he got locked in the booth—the door *should* have opened, but he said it seemed "stuck." For the next several minutes, he heard loud pounding, like someone beating their palms or fists up against the walls from the outside—when he finally got the door open, no one was anywhere to be seen.

She told me that on another occasion, the technicians came in to find the lights above the second stage had been moved around overnight, that instead of pointing at the stage, they were pointing at the ceiling. Not only was the building locked up and empty overnight, but theater lights are big, heavy pieces of equipment. They're also pretty high up off the floor. It takes special equipment and usually a couple of people working together to move them; it certainly couldn't have been the job of a lone prankster.

Finally, Lesley pointed out a door off to the left, behind the seating area, telling me that there have been a number of sightings of an apparition in the doorway. I decided that it would make a good picture for the book—but the brand-new batteries that I had just put in my camera that morning were dead . . . proof? Who knows, but I *had* been saying ever since staying overnight at the Blue Pelican (see Chapter 28) that I would love to experience something a little more "concrete" for myself. Maybe the ghosts of the Baldwin Theatre decided to come out of hiding to grant my wish.

CHAPTER 5

Bone Head's BBQ
WILLIS

I WAS SITTING AROUND with some friends the week after Easter talking about the book I was writing. Everybody knew about the project, knew my deadline was fast approaching, and was excited to hear how it was going. They weren't saying "no" if I happened to offer up a couple of ghost stories, either. One of them even had a ghost story for me.

"We were at Bone Head's BBQ a few months ago," my friend Jayne told me. "And my son *swore* he saw a guy standing by the foot of the stairs leading up to the second floor. When I looked up, I didn't see anything, but when he told our waitress about it, she said it was probably one of the ghosts."

I've known Jayne long enough to consider her reliable, even

if I've never met her teenage son. "So where is this place?" I asked.

She grinned. "Ypsilanti, I think. I can't remember which road—you can probably find it online."

When I got home, I did a quick Internet search and found out that Bone Head's BBQ is actually in Willis, a tiny community that's little more than a dot on the map, just south of Ypsilanti Charter Township. I mapped out my route, packed my gear and an overnight bag, and headed westward on I-94 once again. Willis is actually within easy driving distance of metro-Detroit, but I like to be prepared and was planning a couple of other stops along the way.

I timed my arrival at Bone Head's for lunch because I love BBQ-style food, but I nearly missed my destination and had to turn around. The restaurant did not look like much from the outside, and the town around it consisted of little more than railroad tracks, a post office, and a few streets of older-looking homes. But sometimes the best food is served up in the most out-of-the-way places.

The exterior of the old wood-sided building may have been unimpressive, but as soon as I walked in the door, I knew that I'd come to exactly the right place, both for lunch and ghost stories. The décor was reminiscent of an old general store, the atmosphere was relaxed, and the smells coming from the kitchen were enough to convince me I wouldn't be disappointed. I was greeted by a friendly server and told her that while I was definitely staying for lunch, that wasn't the real reason for my visit. I was writing a book about haunted places and wondered if there might be somebody there who could talk to me about ghosts.

She hesitated a moment before suggesting I should maybe check out their website.

Of course, I would definitely do that when I got back home. "But what I'm really hoping to get are some more personal

stories," I went on. "Anything you've experienced, or maybe
something one of your co-workers or customers have told you."

Over the course of my travels, I've learned that sometimes
I've had to ask more than once. If someone says "no," or "not
interested," I've backed off—some businesses really do not want
a "haunted reputation." But sometimes people have hesitated
either because they weren't sure what I was really asking them
for, or because they didn't want to come off as sounding crazy.
Sometimes just talking to folks for a few minutes was the best
way to get them to open up.

This was one of those times. My waitress looked over at a
woman who was walking through the dining room and asked
her if she had a few minutes to talk to someone writing a book.

The second woman introduced herself as Niki LaChance,
one of the owners. Niki said she had a few minutes, but she was
really in the middle of getting ready for lunch, so she couldn't
talk too long.

"That would be fantastic," I assured her. Before becoming
a full-time writer, I was a full-time waitress, so I completely
understood the restaurant business and that sometimes a few
minutes is all someone has to spare.

Niki refilled her iced tea and showed me over to a table, telling me that she and her husband, Jim, had bought the business
about three years ago. "We opened up on Friday the thirteenth,"
she said.

"That sounds auspicious," I joked.

She laughed too. "It was. Actually, I like to say we came
here by fate," she added. The business had been struggling
before they bought it, but Niki and Jim managed to turn Bone
Head's into a thriving, friendly neighborhood restaurant.
"We're definitely a 'destination location,'" she added, when I
mentioned almost missing the place. "There isn't much else
around here."

Numerous spirits have been spotted by guests on the steps leading upstairs at Bone Head's BBQ.

Niki told me that the village of Willis was named after Willis Potter, one of the area's original landowners. "He came here around 1825."

She took me over to the staircase—the same staircase where my friend's son said he'd seen a ghost—leading up to the second floor to show me some of the old photos hanging on the wall.

"Originally, the building was a stagecoach stop," Niki told me.

She told me that it was built in 1865 and had been the home of many different businesses over the course of the last century and a half. "It was a granary, a butcher shop, an ice house, a post office, a boarding house, and even a general store." Then she went on to tell me that the staircase is one of the most active areas in the restaurant. Maybe that was why I had the chills as we stood on the stairs talking—or was it because I'd already heard about a ghost hanging around the stairwell?

"One of the waitresses told me once that she was standing at the base of the stairs and felt someone touching her hair," said

Niki. "She turned around expecting it to be one of the cooks messing with her—but no one was there.

"The building was completely restored back in the 1980s," Niki went on, emphasizing that it was restored, not renovated. The former owners wanted to recapture the feel of the original building. "They brought in antiques and fixtures from all over the state," she said, pointing out stained glass windows from an old church up north and a huge, old apothecary's cabinet on the far wall filled with antiques.

As she continued telling me about the restaurant's ghosts, it sounded as if more than just antiques were brought into the building when it was restored, however. Besides the man that my friend's son had seen around the staircase, Bone Head's is, according to the staff and customers, haunted by a pair of female specters. One of them is described as a teenage girl, who apparently came into the building along with that apothecary's cabinet. The other female ghost is an older woman they call Nellie, who has, according to Niki, been with the building for as long as anyone could remember. One of the cooks claimed to have seen Nellie walk across the kitchen and out the back door—literally going *through* the door.

"We have a ghost cat, too, named Pickles," said Nikki. "It was . . . 2009, I think. We'd just opened up, and I had a customer ask me why we allowed animals in the dining room. I told him that we *didn't*. He swore he saw a white cat walking along the back wall. Other customers have seen him over the years too."

Niki told me that they've had things like that happening from the very beginning. "One of the first things I personally witnessed was this big vase of flowers sliding right across one of the tables out on the sun porch. I was sitting right over there with three other people." She pointed to a table by the window. "The vase went from the middle of the table right over the edge and broke."

I had to admit, that seemed a little unusual.

"There was another time," Niki went on, "when a lady came out of the restroom really shaken up. I asked her what happened. She told me she'd been standing in front of the mirror—there's a wreath behind the mirrors. One of the glass globes on it just exploded. I made that wreath," she added. "I know how well the ornaments are glued in place. There's no reason for it to have just shattered like that. It didn't fall, it just . . . exploded."

That wasn't the only ghostly encounter someone had had in the ladies' restroom. Another time, Niki told me, one of the waitresses was in there by herself. "She told me that she dropped her cigarette lighter," said Nikki. The lighter must have slid across the floor, because Niki said the waitress told her that as she was bending over to pick it up, it slid back to her, "like somebody had kicked it over to her."

I supposed incidents like that were why Niki categorized the restaurant's spirits as "friendly"—just a little mischievous from time to time. "Sometimes doors open and shut upstairs, or lights flicker. The old owners told me that sometimes the lights would sway back and forth in the bar for seemingly no reason at all," she added.

Then Niki told me that after they bought the place, she asked the former owner if she had ever had any unusual experiences in the restaurant. "She lived in the apartment upstairs," Niki explained. "She said that one morning she came down to get the paper from the front porch. She didn't realize it was raining until she got downstairs, so she went back up to get her slippers. When she came back down, she found the wet newspaper sitting on the inside of the locked front door."

Niki was also told that numerous people have seen "someone" cleaning the front upstairs windows—*after* the former owners moved out, but *before* Niki and her husband bought the

Antique humidor at Bone Head's BBQ.

place and moved into the upstairs apartment with their teenage daughter, Franchesca.

"What's it like living in a haunted building?" I asked.

"At first my daughter was a little nervous—and sometimes it's a little freaky when doors open up upstairs all by themselves. But the first thing I did when we moved in was ask God to watch over us and drive out anything bad. I figured the good spirits could stay, since they were here first. We haven't had any problems; they're just mischievous."

Niki pointed out the clock on the wall and said that it had come with the restaurant, but it had never worked. The previous owners weren't even sure it had "guts" or if it was just decorative.

"Then one night, at exactly eleven-thirty, it started bonging and the minute hand started to move. We were closed up for the night, all the lights were off, and there were just four of us in here. I'd just pulled the cash drawer and was taking it upstairs," she said. "I turned around because I couldn't figure out what the sound was at first. Then I realized it was the clock, and I called to the bartender and my brother-in-law, who were sitting in the bar area talking. I wanted them to see it. My brother-in-law got a chair and took the clock off the wall—all this time it had been bonging," she added. "But as soon as he touched it, it stopped, and suddenly the time read five o'clock. It hasn't made a sound or moved since then.

"And just recently," she went on, "It was about seven-thirty in the morning, and I'd gone out for a run. When I got back, Jim told me that he could have sworn he heard me come in, walk up the stairs, go into the office, and open up the liquor cabinet. The cabinet door squeaks," she explained. "It's a pretty distinctive sound. He wondered what I was doing, so he went into the office—only I wasn't back from my run yet. No one was in the office. The dog heard it too," she added. "Jim told me the dog started barking when he heard the footsteps on the stairs."

Niki said that they'd had a number of paranormal teams come out to investigate the place since they moved in. There have been a lot of orb photos taken as well as EVP (electronic voice phenomena) evidence and video clips, all of which can be accessed from Bone Head's website.

Just about then Patrice, Niki's office manager, came in. Niki called her over and explained what we were talking about, adding that Patrice had accompanied a couple of the paranormal teams when they were at the restaurant doing their investigations.

"Did you tell her about Bob?" Patrice asked.

"No, I almost forgot," said Niki. "Bob used to live in the attic, right at the top of the stairs—it's not much more than a crawl space, but I guess it used to be a bedroom. When the last team was out here they were communicating with him, weren't they?"

Patrice nodded. "I think I remember them saying Bob told them he used to work on the property as some kind of caretaker or maintenance man."

I wondered if maybe that was the apparition my friend's son had seen.

"Have you had any experiences?" Niki asked Patrice.

"Not really . . . well, there was that one time I was sitting here with a friend of mine. She's really sensitive to stuff like this," explained Patrice. "She said she saw a little girl tugging on the apron sting of one of the waitresses."

Later on, when Patrice asked that particular waitress if she'd felt anything unusual that night, the gal told her she'd felt a tugging on her apron string, but had just blown it off as "nothing." Everyone agreed that was a little freaky. I thought so too.

Spotlight On:
The Motor City Ghost Hunters

Last September I visited the Whitefish Point Lighthouse and Shipwreck Museum. Just as I was pulling in, the Motor City Ghost Hunters were pulling out. But before they could hit the road for the long trek back home, Beth, the housekeeper for the Crew Quarters at Whitefish Point, introduced us. I couldn't have met with a nicer or more knowledgeable group of people.

As I was wrapping up the last details of this book, I got back in touch with John, who is both the team's leader and founder, to thank him again for taking the time to talk with me that day back in September and to ask permission to use some of the information from their website to put together a "Team Profile" for my book. He graciously gave me the go-ahead and filled me in on some of the things they've been up to since the last time we spoke.

Probably the most exciting news is that when the Ghost Hunters were going over their footage from Whitefish Point, they realized they'd caught what looks like an apparition on tape. Fox News ran the clip; it can also be seen on both the Ghost Hunters' website and on YouTube. John told me the footage has been turned over to SyFy's *Fact or Faked* for further investigation—but he was there that night and assured me that there was nothing "fake" about it. Not that I thought there might be. The Ghost Hunters may be believers in the paranormal, but they will always look for logical explanations first.

John said he and his teammates have been on investigations pretty much every weekend since September and have a lot more planned for the coming year, including visits to the Mansfield State Prison, Yankee Air Museum, and, of course, their annual visit to Whitefish Point. Also included in their busy schedule are a number of educational talks at local libraries, as well as a special event just for children who are interested in learning more about the paranormal.

John told me that he and his team always put children first, and any request for an investigation where kids are involved will always get top priority. "It's about letting people know they don't have to be afraid, especially in their own home or business," he said. The sentiment is echoed by every other member of the team. That desire to ease people's fears is what drives these folks to give up their weekends and free time, because none of them are paid for what they do—yet they give up countless hours and spend no small amount of money on equipment. Having talked to them at length the day we met and speaking to John again on the phone, it was easy to see why the Motor City Ghost Hunters are so well respected.

John is a licensed mechanical contractor with certification in microbial pest management. In other words, he's pretty good at figuring out if what seems to be a ghostly phenomenon is "real" or if it can easily be explained away as something related to the structure of a building. Like many of his teammates, he has been interested in the paranormal for most of his life.

One of the other members I met at Whitefish Point was Chass. Like John, she's married with children and has experienced a number of things in her life that couldn't be easily or scientifically explained. Chass joined the team after the Motor City Ghost Hunters conducted an investigation in her home.

I also met lead investigator and case manager Kellie, who describes herself as both a "true believer" and a bit of a skeptic. Her educational background is in social science.

Of course, with more than two dozen team members, it would be impossible to mention them all, or even the half dozen or so I was fortunate to meet at Whitefish Point. What I can say is that I look forward to seeing them again; I've been invited to join them on an investigation and have every intention of accepting that invitation as soon as time allows.

CHAPTER 6

Battle Alley Arcade Antiques Mall
HOLLY

HOLLY IS PERHAPS BEST KNOWN as the home of the Michigan Renaissance Festival, a favorite autumn destination for Michiganders of all ages, and for the Mt. Holly Ski and Snowboard Resort, one of Lower Michigan's most popular winter retreats. Another reason to visit the village of Holly is the annual Dickens Festival, held each December along the town's historic downtown district. The festival brings Charles Dickens's *A Christmas Carol* to life by recreating a truly old-fashioned Christmas with carolers, a tree-lighting ceremony, and, of course, a visit from Father Christmas (or simply "Santa" to most American children). But if you're a paranormal investigator or, like me, just an amateur ghosthunter in search of a few good stories, you will find a lot more than the spirits of Christmas past haunting the quiet 160-year-old village. Holly is said by some to be one of the most haunted little towns in Michigan—which meant I was really looking forward to my visit. I took my husband along with me for this trip too, although I think he was more interested in preventing me from shopping too much than he was in any ghost stories.

Our first stop was the Battle Alley Antiques Arcade, located next door to the historic Holly Hotel. Since it was pretty close to the holiday season, I had called ahead and made an appointment with the antiques shop owner, Patricia Kenny. Pat graciously agreed to show me around and talk to me about the arcade's history and resident spirits, as long as I came up on a weekday. That worked for us, and I told Pat I would be there on Monday.

When my husband got home from work that afternoon, we made some hot cocoa for the road, bundled up, and were on our way. Holly isn't far from us, less than an hour, and it was a nice day for a drive and maybe a little holiday shopping—or at least pointing out to my husband all the things I might like to find in *my* stocking this year! Street parking in downtown Holly proved to be a bit sparse, but my husband found us a spot a short distance from the antiques arcade. We enjoyed a short walk through the historic district, where all of the stores were decked with evergreen garland and red velvet bows for the upcoming holiday season.

I had been curious about how the street named Battle Alley got its name. We found a plaque in downtown Holly that told us the story: Holly hasn't always been the peaceful little village it is today; it started out as a railroad town, filled with migrant workers and their families, as well as the occasional farmer who would come in for supplies. Despite the fact that Oakland County, in which Holly is situated, was a "dry" county at the turn of the 20th century, the village of Holly maintained a number of saloons and speakeasies in its downtown district. In 1880, a skirmish broke out between some of the migrant railway workers who had settled in Holly and a troupe of travelling circus performers. The fight was said to have left so many people injured that the street on which the brawl took place was dubbed "Battle Alley," and the name stuck, even into modern times.

Apparently, the drunk and disorderly conduct continued, because in 1908 the Holly prohibition committee called in the infamous Kansas saloon smasher, Carry A. Nation, to put an end to the town's alcohol problems. After taking her trademark axe to the liquor shelves of the Holly Hotel's saloon, however, Ms. Nation found *herself* under arrest. Her conduct may not have been drunken, but town officials decided it was most certainly disorderly!

In 1975, Holly established the Carry Nation Festival to celebrate Ms. Nation's visit to the village. It may not be as well known as the Renaissance or Dickens Festivals, but the Carry Nation Festival commemorates an important chapter of Holly's history. In addition to the usual festival traditions—a parade, pageant, and reenactment of Ms. Nation's visit to the village— many of the downtown pubs offer guests special menus and reduced prices on drinks. Clearly, the residents of Holly have a good sense of humor about their colorful past.

In short order, my husband and I reached our destination, a two-story white brick storefront. Stepping into the Battle Alley Antiques Arcade was more like stepping out onto a Victorian-era street than it was like stepping into an antiques shop. Rather than the usual setup of booths or row after row of display cases, visitors find actual small "shops" lining each side of a long walkway. More than 20 antiques dealers call the arcade home; you can find everything from old vinyl records to antique furniture, vintage clothes, jewelry, and dolls.

"Swaying lights" at the Battle Alley Arcade.

My husband and I were greeted by Patricia Kenny and her brother John, who run the antiques arcade. After making our introductions, Pat invited me to step into a quieter corner of the shop so we could talk. She was candid about her shop's ghosts. "What would you like to know?" she asked right off the bat.

As usual, I didn't have any prepared questions. I prefer to invite people to talk to me about their experiences, anything they've seen or heard themselves, or anything guests or customers have reported. I asked Pat to tell me about the shop's ghosts.

"We're very haunted," she began. "A lot of buildings in Holly are. We've had a number of paranormal investigators come out to see us." Pat went on to tell me that the Motor City Ghost Hunters had recently been out for another visit, and she was looking forward to getting the full report as soon as they were done reviewing their findings. They'd already sent her a couple of preliminary photographs and let her hear a few audio recordings, and the evidence seemed tantalizing. "You can hear a little boy saying 'buy it for me, Mommy' really clearly on one of the recordings they made upstairs."

I was curious about how and why she'd contacted the Motor City Ghost Hunters to come up in the first place. "Did you call them?" I asked. "Or did they hear about you being haunted and ask if they could come out?"

"They were up here conducting an investigation at the Holly Hotel," she explained, "and came next door to see us too." Pat told me that when the Ghost Hunters came into her shop, one of their sensitives said she felt the presence of their resident ghost cat. "It brushes up against peoples' legs," Pat told me. "My brother John has even felt it." The ghost cat was the very first spirit Pat said a psychic had told her about, some 15 years ago.

But the ghostly feline isn't the only spirit who inhabits the arcade. Pat told me that customers are always telling her how they see shadows out of the corners of their eyes or feel as if they are being watched. "Make sure you go upstairs," she added. Apparently, the second floor of the Antiques Arcade has seen some pretty interesting activity. "I remember one day a gentleman came down the steps pretty quickly and left without a word. It was a little odd, but I didn't think that much of it until later when I went across the street to get some lunch. They asked me what I was doing to my customers over here. The man I'd seen rushing out the door had ended up across the street and was really shaken up." Later, the customer returned and told Pat that he'd been upstairs and someone came up behind him and knocked his hat from his head.

Except there *wasn't* anyone else upstairs at the time.

Of course, not everyone who visits the arcade believes in ghosts; not all of the vendors do, either. That doesn't make them immune to unusual phenomena, however. Pat told me that one morning one of the antiques dealers was opening the arcade up for the day—"he doesn't believe in any of this," she added with a smile. "He follows the same routine every time he opens up. He always walks down and gets all the lights on this side, then turns on the lights on the other side on his way back to the front of the store." She had me follow her down the long, narrow path down the middle of the arcade so I could see for myself. It's a fairly long walk from the front of the store to the back of it. "It was first thing in the morning, and no one else was back here," she said, as we got to the rear of the arcade. "But he told me that when he got back here, that light was swinging back and forth." She pointed to the middle light in a row of three hanging from the ceiling in a rear booth area. The light is high up, definitely over my head; even a tall man would not have been able to reach it without a ladder. But, as Pat had just said, there was no one else in the store.

"This area has a lot of activity," she told me of that particular room. "One morning another vendor was back here opening up, and she said she heard fabric rustling behind her, like a woman's long skirt. When she turned around, no one was there. She hurried back up to the front to wait for her daughter to come in. She didn't want to be back here alone."

Just like most of the people I'd talked to over the last few months, Pat said she wasn't at all uncomfortable working in such a haunted environment. For her, spirits are just a part of the day-to-day operation of an antiques store. "Whenever a new vendor comes in, or someone moves things around in their shop, it always seems to stir things up," she told me. "Old furniture, mirrors, and especially dolls have spirits connected to them," she added.

But it's not just the antiques at the Battle Alley Arcade that attract spirits. The building material used to decorate the interior was donated from numerous older sites to create the unique layout of the mall. Old fixtures, beams, shutters, and other odds and ends adorn the arcade's interior and attract spirits as much as the antiques themselves do—at least according to people who believe in ghosts and other paranormal phenomena. The theory is that spirits attach themselves to items that were important to them in life. That may be why ghosts are so often attached to dolls; who is more possessive of a favorite toy than a child?

The arcade is structurally old as well and has had an interesting history. Pat told me that the back part of the building was built around 1916 or 1917 and was called the Liberty Theatre. By 1927, it was called the Liberty Theatre and Confectionery. "Part of the building used to be connected to the hotel, next door," Pat told me. I discovered later that at that time the Holly Hotel was running a speakeasy, and the arcade was home to a brothel. I don't know about the ghosts, but if the walls could only talk I imagine they would have some interesting stories to tell.

While we were walking around the shop, Pat pointed out a few of the places paranormal investigators have gotten some of their best evidence, and she showed me one of the photographs the Motor City Ghost Hunters emailed to her after their most recent visit. You can find it on their website and decide for yourself if the reflection in the glass display case is really a human figure or just an optical illusion. According to the accompanying report, the reflection isn't of anyone who was in the room at the time, nor was there anything near the case that could have been responsible for a human-shaped reflection.

I took a picture of the same case but didn't see anything unusual. Oh, well, maybe next time.

Before I left, Pat gave me the name of another shop in town, Main Street Antiques, and said I would be sure to get in touch with Lynn and Mark to talk about their ghosts too.

But that's another story. . . .

CHAPTER 7

Main Street Antiques
HOLLY

IT WAS A SHORT WALK from the Battle Alley Arcade down to the Main Street Antiques Shop, a store that has been a mainstay of downtown Holly for many years. It's also one of the oldest buildings in Holly's historic district. In 2008, Lynn and Mark Hay purchased the business, and they happily agreed to talk to me about their shop and its resident ghosts.

The two-story, red-brick shop is home to 40 antiques dealers selling a wild variety of heirlooms, antiques, artifacts, and collectables, including some rather unusual merchandise. The first thing my husband spotted when we walked in the door was a vampire slaying kit. The kit, which Lynn speculates originated somewhere in Europe, contained rosaries, holy water, wooden stakes, a mallet, and even a revolver loaded with actual silver bullets. Leave it to my husband to find the strangest thing in the shop!

Lynn told me sometimes she feels like her shop is "a magnet for the unusual." In addition to the vampire slaying kit, she has had numerous Native American items and even real shrunken heads come into her store over the years. Looking around the store, it wasn't hard to find a few curiosities tucked in amongst the teacups, antique buttons, and costume jewelry. It was no wonder that prop masters from six movie production teams have visited Lynn and Mark's shop to find just that "perfect piece" to complete a movie set.

The only things Lynn told me she would not allow in her shop were Ouija boards and tarot cards. She explained that she believed in the paranormal and that there were both good and bad spirits out there, but that certain items just naturally attract energy she didn't want around her. I had heard before how dangerous Ouija boards were because they somehow attracted malicious spirits. I had a friend many years ago who was absolutely petrified of "witch boards," as they are sometimes called.

Other people, of course, dismiss the boards as nothing more than hoaxes or parlor games. As for tarot cards, Lynn couldn't imagine why anyone would want to read with used tarot cards, anyway. "You never know the kind of person who owned them before you," she said.

After we chatted for a few minutes, Lynn invited my husband and me to follow her up to the second floor, where we could find a quieter place to talk. She led the way up the narrow wooden staircase, at the top of which sits a portrait of a little girl.

"A lot of people say they see a little girl running around up here," Lynn told me. "And we all hear footsteps coming from up here, like someone's walking around, even though there isn't anyone up here." She directed us to a corner by the windows overlooking Main Street, where she cleared the place settings off a seventies-era wooden dinette table so we could sit and talk more comfortably.

I asked her a little bit about the shop.

"Mark has been in the antique business for a long time," said Lynn. "So when we found out that this place was for rent and that the owners wanted it to remain an antiques shop, it just seemed like the right move to make.

"Antiques attract spirits; they get attached to them," she went on, echoing what Pat Kenny from the Battle Alley Arcade had told me already. "Whenever something from a new dealer comes in, we notice a lot more activity. It's like the ghosts who have been here awhile feel like they need to 'check out' the new guys." Lynn has also noticed that spirits seem attracted to dolls and mirrors.

Another reason the shop might be so haunted, she speculated, is that the downstairs was "where they used to wash down the hearses" in the late 1800s when the building was owned by a wagon company.

"When did you first start to notice things that made you think the store might be haunted?" I asked.

"As soon as we moved in," she said. She explained that shortly after they set up shop, she and her husband would notice that things seemed to have been moved around overnight. They were both certain they had locked up the night before, and no one else should have had keys. Nothing was stolen; things just weren't where they remembered them being the night before— nothing huge, just small objects. "It looked almost like someone was cleaning up," she said. Neither Lynn nor Mark could imagine anyone breaking in to clean, but they went ahead and changed the locks anyway, just to be on the safe side.

Small objects continued to get moved overnight. Then, one winter morning, Lynn discovered something far more

Haunted "white room" at Main Street Antiques.

bewildering than just a few items moved around. "The city puts salt out on the sidewalks during the winter months," she explained. "It gets on peoples' shoes and they track it in, where it gets all over the hardwood floors. Usually we clean it up at night before we go home, but that particular evening we were just too tired to sweep up. Mark and I decided to come in a little early the next morning and clean it then. Only when we came in the next day, we found fresh footprints all through the white salty residue. They *hadn't* been there the night before, and I *know* I locked the door when we left that night," she concluded emphatically.

Lynn said she thinks the spirit may be the ghost of someone who used to work in the store; the building has been an antiques shop for many years, long before she and Mark bought the place. "She—or maybe he—is just cleaning up the way they did when they were alive and worked here." We should all have ghosts who are so helpful!

But not all the spirits who seem to haunt Main Street Antiques are as benevolent as their ghostly shop assistant. When I asked Lynn what her favorite ghost story was, she had to stop and think a minute because she had seen and heard so many things in the four years she and her husband have owned her shop. "I don't know if it's my *favorite* story," she began thoughtfully, "but one of the freakiest things I ever saw happened downstairs on that yellow ramp, right after we moved in." The first floor of the shop isn't just one big room—although the main room is impressively large. However, in addition, there are a number of smaller, adjacent rooms, and one of them has a bright yellow ramp leading up to it (thus making it wheelchair accessible).

What Lynn told me she'd seen there would have been enough to make me turn around and run out the door.

"I walked in and I saw this headless guy, flailing around, right on the ramp. It was like something you'd see in a movie or something. His movements were real fast and jerky, and he looked like maybe he'd been burned."

"What did you do?"

"I just took a deep breath and waited for him to go away." Lynn told me she's found that if she doesn't pay too much attention to them, the ghosts don't usually stick around for long. I don't think I could have been so calm.

"There was a fire here," she went on to explain. "They think it was arson and that the arsonist died in the blaze. The ghost I saw was probably him." She hasn't seen him since. Many people believe that when a person dies violently, their spirit somehow gets tied to the place where they died.

Besides the headless arsonist, Lynn told me about some of the apparitions that numerous people have seen. "There's a woman that people have seen walking through a closed door downstairs," Lynn told me—and later she pointed out the door. Other customers have reported seeing a man in a top hat, dressed as if he's going out for a night on the town. Lynn told me to make sure that I checked out the "white room" when I went back downstairs, as it is also one of the more reputedly haunted areas of the shop.

One night, Lynn decided to conduct her own investigation of the shop, with the help of some friends. "We kept hearing a little girl's voice over the walkie-talkies. It definitely wasn't one of us, so at first we thought we might be picking up something from outside." Walkie-talkies can pick up radio signals pretty easily. "But then the voice started saying our names. It was pretty freaky and it convinced us that whatever we have here, it's real." Not that Lynn needed much convincing; she told me she had always believed in the paranormal.

Like many of the residents of Holly, Lynn believes that the whole village is haunted. "It's such an old town, and so many people have lived and died here," she said. She told me that she and her family had experienced a number of unusual things in their home as well, and that later, when she started looking into the history of the shop, she discovered a connection between the house they're renting and the store. Apparently, many years ago, long before the previous owners purchased either building, both the antiques store and her home were owned by the same family.

"Is there a place in the shop that seems the most haunted?" I asked.

"Definitely up here. When customers tell me they feel like they're being watched upstairs, I usually tell them it's just the security cameras—but not all of them believe me. Some people are just more sensitive to spirits than others. We have some customers that won't even come up here anymore."

It's not just customers. Lynn told me how one of the antiques dealers who used to have a spot in the corner came to her one day and asked if she could bring a radio in. She told Lynn that she kept hearing scratching along the floorboards and it was really unnerving. If she had music, she wouldn't have to listen to it anymore.

Lynn had no objection to the radio. When she checked the floorboards later, she couldn't find scratch marks; there wasn't any evidence of vermin, mice, or rats that might have been responsible for the scratching either.

There's another part of the upstairs that is blocked off to customers; I had thought it was just an old storage area, but Lynn told me that the ghost she saw in there unsettled her so badly that she decided to close off the room. She said he smelled strongly of tar and was wearing soiled clothing. He didn't do anything, but Lynn said she felt his presence was "disturbing." Considering the things she took in stride, I was just as glad that area of her shop was blocked off.

Lynn said she thought the tar-smelling ghost might have been a railway worker, since Holly was originally a railroad town. I thanked Lynn for her time and hospitality and went off to wander the shop with my husband and take some photographs before heading to the Holly Hotel.

Spotlight On: Dunn's Tomb

I probably shouldn't admit to how much personal experience I have with this particular location, but I was one of those kids who visited Dunn's Tomb regularly as a teenager. My friends and I never actually did anything when we went to the old cemetery, except try to scare underclassmen with tales of mad monks and rabid German shepherds, but we probably shouldn't have been there. Truthfully, I'd forgotten about my miscreant youth until I was talking with an old friend from high school and the subject of *Ghosthunting Michigan* came up.

"You're going to write about Dunn's Tomb, aren't you?" Frank asked. "Oh, you have to!"

He was right. I do have to write about it, not because of my own adventures, but because Dunn's Tomb is one of Oakland County's most famous allegedly haunted places. Not that I ever saw any ghosts there, or any evidence of mad monks either, although there really is a monastery nearby. Dunn's Tomb is located in the Lakeville Cemetery off of Drahner Road. The remote location is made even scarier (at least to a bunch of teenagers) by its close proximity to the Addison Oaks Country Park, a large overgrown nature preserve. The tomb has always reminded me of a burial mound more than any sort of mausoleum, and is located in a remote part of the cemetery off one of the older paths. Unfortunately, that hasn't stopped vandals from frequenting the area.

There doesn't seem to be just one single story connected to Dunn's Tomb, but rather a whole collection of them. In one tale, a pair of teenagers, a boy and a girl, were dared by friends to spend the night in the old hillside mausoleum. When their friends returned the next day, the pair was dead, but there was no obvious cause of death. It is said that if you happen to drive to the cemetery in a black car, you can park by the fence late at night and eventually you'll see the ghostly pair hovering nearby. Apparently, the friends who dropped them off and came to fetch them again the next morning were in a black car, and the teens are still looking for their ride home.

Another story says that visitors to the tomb return to their vehicle to find ghostly handprints on the windshield, as if someone had been touching their car, perhaps trying to get in.

In another story, a man got locked in the tomb overnight, went mad, and killed himself. In another version, rather than committing suicide, the madman became an ax murderer and kept his victims' bodies in the tomb.

None of those stories have ever been verified—and most of them are probably patently false. What is known about Dunn's Tomb is that it contains the earthly remains of James and Elizabeth Dunn. Mr. Dunn died in 1930; his wife passed away in 1952. Despite the wild stories told about the tomb, which might lead a person to discount that there's any kernel of truth hiding at the center of the legends, a number of paranormal investigators have been to the area and claim to have gotten compelling evidence that leads them to believe that someone—or something—haunts the area.

CHAPTER 8

Holly Hotel
HOLLY

THE HISTORIC HOLLY HOTEL is said to be the single most haunted building in the state of Michigan. It has been written about in newspapers and magazines and has been featured on both local and national television. In 2009, it was the subject of an episode of the popular Travel Channel program, "The Most Terrifying Places in America." Numerous paranormal investigators have visited the Holly Hotel, including the Motor City Ghost Hunters, the Ghost Hunters of Southern Michigan, the Michigan Paranormal Research Association, and well-known parapsychologist Norman Gauthier, who concluded that the building was "loaded with spirits." Of the places that I'd planned to visit in Holly, this was the one I'd been looking the most forward to—but not just for the ghosts.

Despite its name, the Holly Hotel is no longer an inn and does not accommodate overnight guests. However, the dining room remains a favorite spot for dinner, afternoon tea, and Sunday brunch. Dinner is served nightly, while a traditional Victorian-style high tea is served every day except for Sunday. The restaurant's menu is an award-winning blend of traditional signature dishes, some of which have changed very little over the last century, and contemporary seasonal fare. In addition to being featured in magazines and on television for its ghosts, the Holly Hotel is known nationally for its fine cuisine. So, having saved the "best for last," my husband and I headed back down Broad Street to the historic Holly Hotel to have dinner.

We enjoyed an early meal and stuck around to catch the show at the Holly Hotel Comedy Club, which has been a featured part of the venue since the early 1980s. I figured I owed him a proper night out after all his patience the previous week, not to mention dragging him around to antiques shops with me. Built in 1891, the Holly Hotel was originally known as the Hirst Hotel, named after proprietor John Hirst. In those days, it was a "railway inn," one of many hotels constructed along the railway lines around the turn of the century. At that time, almost two dozen trains passed in and out of Holly each day, bringing with them travelers, railway workers, transients, and supplies. Saloons lined Martha Street to accommodate travelers, but so many brawls broke out in the saloon district that the street was soon dubbed "Battle Alley." The name stuck and eventually became official.

It is on the corner of Broad Street and Battle Alley that you'll find the Holly Hotel, a stately three-story, red-brick, Queen Anne–style building. The hotel dominates the block and continues to be a cornerstone of Holly's social life, just as it was at the turn of the century—although it has a far less seedy reputation than in the days of saloons, bar brawls, and brothels.

The inn's most famous ghost is probably Mr. Hirst himself, who passed away in the 1920s, but who, many believe, has never let go of his hotel. He is reputed to be the most active—and most unhappy—when renovations have been made to the property. A myriad of other spirits are said to inhabit the 120-year-old building.

After dinner, I asked our waiter about the hotel's history and its haunted reputation. He said he'd heard there were supposed to be ghosts, but he hadn't been there long enough to experience anything out of the ordinary for himself.

"Did you know it was supposed to be one of the most haunted places in the state before you applied here?" I asked.

"I'd heard stories—everyone in Holly has. But I never ran into anybody who was afraid to work here or anything. The ghosts are just a part of the place, I guess."

He invited me to get in touch with owner and chef, George Kutlenios, if I wanted to know more. George wasn't in, so I would have to email him to arrange a time to talk later, but in the meantime, I was free to have a look around the public areas and talk to other employees. Several staff members told me that they'd experienced cold spots in different places around the building and smelled cigar smoke in empty rooms—apparently the late Mr. Hirst was a heavy cigar smoker.

Another staff member said that one night when she was closing up, she heard footsteps on the staircase behind her.

"I turned around to see who it was, I was *sure* no one else was upstairs. And there wasn't! There was no one there." We both started getting goose bumps as she was talking about it.

She told me she thought it was the spirit of a little girl who died on the premises after having been injured in the stables that were once adjacent to the building, where the parking lot now stands. "It's probably the same little girl who plays in the kitchen sometimes," she added.

I left with some interesting tidbits and was eager to get more information. As soon as I got home, I dropped George an email; he responded a few days later to tell me that the person I should speak to was Alex Cripps, one of the hotel managers who, in George's words, "is the most knowledgeable person" on staff when it came to the Holly Hotel's ghosts.

In the meantime, I'd done some more research of my own and discovered that the Holly Hotel suffered two major fires in its long history. The first occurred on January 19, 1913, and the second was 65 years later on January 19, 1878. Reports have it that both fires started at "exactly the same time, to the hour." I also discovered that if I'd visited the Holly Hotel in October, I may have been able to attend a séance or "ghost hunt" (of course, there's always next year!). Reservations are highly recommended for anyone wishing to attend one of the Holly Hotel's special haunted activities, as spaces fill up fast.

After playing a bit of phone tag, Alex and I were finally able to connect, and he was happy to share with me some of the things he has been told about and experienced firsthand over the years as a server and manager in the building. One of the most startling pieces of evidence Alex said that he had ever seen was a photograph taken during a customer's 21st birthday party. One of the guests took the photo using an iPhone without a flash. On the wall behind the table hung a mirror, and reflected in the mirror was the image of a woman that was so clear, most people looking at the photo think it is a portrait. The mirror has an ornate frame, much like a picture frame, but Alex assured me it really is a mirror—and I was pretty sure I remembered passing the mirror myself when I was touring the hotel on my previous visit. Like most of the staff members I had spoken to before, Alex has experienced cold spots throughout the building. He said he especially notices them in the summer.

"And sometimes I just walk into a room and get goose bumps for no reason, or see a flicker of movement out of the corner of my eye, but when I turn around, there's nothing there," he added. Alex said he'd heard that peripheral vision was better for seeing ghosts. "Your brain doesn't analyze what you see out of the corner of your eye the same way it analyzes things you see head on."

He went on to tell me about an experience one of the servers had related to him about their "Dining Car Room," which was renovated to look like an authentic 1940s railway dining car.

"A lot of people have had unusual experiences in that room, but this one was really interesting," Alex began. "There was a family eating dinner, but the little boy with them was really quiet. Not just normal 'well-behaved child' quiet, but almost withdrawn." He went on to explain how the waitress tried to bring the boy out of his shell a little, talking to him and being friendly, but the boy remained aloof. "Finally the grandmother apologized for the boy. She told the server that he's really sensitive to spirits and had probably seen something."

On another occasion, a customer reported seeing the ghostly apparition of a woman in the same room.

In fact, the Holly Hotel has been the sighting of a number of apparitions over the years. One of the most frequently seen is believed to be the spirit of Nora Kane, a former hostess of the inn. Many guests claim to have seen her in the bar area and in the back hallway, which used to be the main entrance to the hotel. Some people think that Ms. Kane is especially drawn to weddings and parties—perhaps it was her image that was captured on camera by the guest with the iPhone. Her perfume, a sweet floral scent, has been noticed by both staff members and visitors alike, and many people believe it is she they have heard singing from time to time, in otherwise empty rooms.

Alex told me that the manager before him swore he heard someone talking to him one morning, even though there was no one else in the hotel. "He told me it was early morning and he'd come in to get some work done before the restaurant opened up. He was sitting in the office and heard someone call out his name. When he went to find out who else was in the building, he couldn't find anyone."

Alex concluded by telling me he suspects that part of the reason Holly seems to be more haunted than some other cities is that it's such a small town and that folks there are generally open-minded. It makes sense. I've read in other places that one of the reasons paranormal researchers believe children are more apt to see spirits and other phenomena is that they are more open-minded than adults—they don't yet believe that "there's no such thing as ghosts."

CHAPTER 9

Fenton Hotel Tavern & Grille
FENTON

DESPITE ITS NAME, the Fenton Hotel hasn't been an actual inn since the 1950s.

Originally constructed in 1856, the stately, three-story brick building on the corner of Main Street and Leroy in downtown Fenton has changed hands, and names, numerous times over the last 150 years. Even so, the place retains much of its former beauty—at least on the first floor. The second and third floors are another matter. The former guest rooms have fallen into disuse, and while there is some office space upstairs as well as some storage areas, most of the upper two floors of the former hotel are completely closed off—which doesn't stop people from swearing that sometimes they hear someone, or some*thing*, walking around up there. Or so the stories go.

I arrived at the Fenton Hotel on a rainy Friday night, which probably wasn't the best time to show up at a restaurant asking about their ghosts, but it was my only night that week. Margaret Perry, who has been with the Fenton Hotel for nine years, greeted me at the hostess stand. She was the perfect person to talk to, but she was also extremely busy. I was grateful to her for taking a few minutes for me in between shepherding customers to their tables. One of the things I was most struck by as I watched Margaret working was how well she and the other staff members knew their customers. Over half of the guests who came in were greeted by name as staff members asked about their spouses, grandchildren, recent vacations, or fishing trips.

I had a few minutes to glance over the menu, which was classic American fare; probably if they weren't so busy, I would have stayed for dinner, but there truly wasn't a table to be had. So instead, I waited patiently by the hostess stand for Margaret to get back to me.

"Sorry about that," she said, returning once more.

It was absolutely no problem.

After catching her breath and collecting her thoughts for a second, Margaret told me about her first encounter with the Fenton Hotel's ghostly entities. She said that when she was a new employee, she remembered standing at the hostess stand and feeling something brush against her ankles. She was pretty unnerved and started looking around, wondering if maybe a mouse had somehow gotten in, but she couldn't see anything. She kept a keen eye out, but continued to see no signs of vermin.

Later on that night, one of the servers was up at the hostess stand and grumbled, "Those darned ghosts! They won't leave my ankles alone tonight!"

Perhaps it was the ghostly black cat that some believe wanders the building. Other ghosts said to inhabit the hotel-turned-tavern include a mysterious man who is occasionally observed sitting at a table in the dining room—table number 32, according to several witnesses. Even Margaret said she'd seen him once or twice.

"I was walking past that doorway there," she said, indicating the doorway between the dining room and foyer, "and thought I saw someone sitting at one of the tables, out of the corner of my eye. There shouldn't have been anyone in there—and when I blinked, he was gone."

She also told me that just the previous weekend, she came in and thought she saw a man sitting on the sofa in the foyer. She went about her business for a few minutes, and when she looked back up, the man was gone.

"It happened to me, like, three times that night. Finally, I asked my manager 'Did you see anybody sitting in the foyer?' She said, 'No, why?' and I told her what I'd seen. She hadn't seen him." Margaret shrugged. "I guess I'm not 100 percent sure I saw someone; I was pretty tired that night, but. . . ." she said, her voice trailing off.

After seating a couple of customers who had come in out of the rain, Margaret told me another story.

"I was standing over by the service bar," she said—the service bar is where the wait staff orders drinks for their tables. "And I heard a man right behind me. His voice was so clear, and he said very politely 'Pardon me.' I turned around expecting to see someone trying to get past—but there was no one there."

Margaret told me about another time when she was sitting alone in the dining room eating her own dinner and saw what looked like smoke moving across the room. At first she wondered if it was cigarette smoke, though it seemed unlikely as smoking isn't allowed in Michigan restaurants any more.

"Then I saw what looked like lights, or orbs, in the smoke—now, the first thing I thought was that it was just light reflecting in from the window or something," she clarified. "But then I realized that it wasn't. I can't explain what I saw, but around here, there's a lot of that."

She told me, "We hear running around up on the second floor all the time."

Both guests and employees have also reported hearing a baby crying, when there weren't any children around, or that doors seem to shut all by themselves. There have been numerous reports of glasses mysteriously falling off shelves in the bar. Margaret personally recently witnessed a martini glass break "for no apparent reason."

"It just fell over and broke," she told me.

In fact, many people believe that the bar of the Fenton Hotel may be the most haunted part of the tavern, although other people will tell you it's the ladies' room, where many customers have reported experiencing an "eerie feeling," or even having their hair and clothing tugged on. Rumor has it that around the turn of the century, a young woman hanged herself in the hotel. She is usually described as a "working girl" who was renting one of the rooms on the hotel's third floor. The story goes that she became pregnant out of wedlock and was so distraught over her situation that she took her own life, quite possibly in the ladies' restroom on the main floor. The rumor has never been substantiated, however.

While Margaret was on the phone taking a reservation, a man and woman came in. They asked me if I was waiting to be seated, but I said that no, I was writing a book about historic buildings in Michigan and that Margaret was helping me out with stories about the Fenton Hotel.

"Oh, are you writing about the ghosts?" the woman asked me.

I told her that yes, I was.

"Tell her about the time we heard that man's voice coming out of the speaker in the bar," the woman urged her companion.

He looked a little sheepish. "It was probably nothing," he said.

"We heard a man's voice singing along with the music coming out of the speakers in the bar," the woman insisted.

By then, Margaret was off the phone; apparently undeterred by their prior experiences, the couple asked for a seat in the bar if there was room.

"People certainly don't seem afraid here," I remarked to Margaret when she got back to the hostess stand.

She smiled. "No, it's just part of our charm."

Perhaps the most famous of the Fenton Hotel's ghosts is Emery, the former caretaker of the inn. Little seems to be known about Emery, other than that he once lived upstairs in a small second-floor bedroom and that he still haunts the second floor. He is the spirit who is believed to roam the second floor. He has been known to knock on the floor and walls after closing, and some staff members and customers believe he even picks up the telephone from time to time.

However, while you will probably be able to get the staff and other guests to talk to you about Emery and rest of the Fenton Hotel's ghosts, the owners Nick and Peggy Sorise have become less willing to deal with their ghosts in recent years. It doesn't seem to be so much a case of fearing bad publicity as much as the Sorises are just busy trying to run their business and don't have the time to escort investigators around on the upper floors.

Spotlight On: Greenfield Village and Henry Ford Museum

If people like Lynn from Main Street Antiques and Pat from the Battle Alley Arcade are right, then the more pieces of old furniture or old building materials you have around, the greater your chances are of having ghosts—assuming you believe in ghosts. Many of the other people I've spoken to in the course of writing this book have also said they have noticed how paranormal activity seemed to increase when they brought antiques into their businesses. So it stands to reason that a place like Dearborn's Greenfield Village and Henry Ford Museum, which is nothing but antiques and old homes, would be teeming with paranormal activity. And according to a lot of people, it is.

Greenfield Village and the Henry Ford Museum is a legacy left to us by the museum's namesake, automotive giant Henry Ford. Ford's passion for preserving American history and culture led him to amass, preserve, and exhibit more than 90 acres' worth of historically significant Americana, including large exhibits like Thomas Edison's laboratory, the Wright Brothers' bicycle shop, and many historic homes, including the Firestone Farm, which was originally constructed in 1828 in Columbiana, Ohio. Other permanent exhibits include John F. Kennedy's presidential limousine, the chair Abraham Lincoln was assassinated in, and the bus made famous by Rosa Parks. The folks who run Greenfield Village are more interested in traditional history than in paranormal activity, but several places around the village are reputed to be haunted, including the Firestone Farm, the Dagget Farm, William Ford Barn, and the Wright Brothers' home—at least according to former employees of the Village.

On the Firestone Farm, it is said that one can hear Sally Firestone walking around upstairs. Her bedroom is said to be particularly active; sometimes she can even be seen peering out the window.

Former employees have reported they would find the drapes pulled back and furniture out of place in the room. Equine specters are said to stamp their hooves in the William Ford Barn, and in the Wright Brothers' family home, people claim to have seen Katherine Wright, the famous pair's younger sister. At the Dagget Farm, some people have claimed to catch a whiff of pipe smoke, particularly in the autumn months. Most of the Village's supposedly paranormal activity happens at night, and management tends to be closed-mouthed about it. But if you ask around discretely, you might be able to get some of the employees to tell you a ghost story or two.

Thumb Area

Bay Port
Sweet Dreams Inn Victorian Bed & Breakfast

Forester Township
Forester Township Cemetery

Lapeer
Castaways Food & Spirits

Memphis
Boomers Tavern

Richmond
Time on Main Euro Café

CHAPTER 10

Castaways Food & Spirits
LAPEER

MY GRANDMOTHER USED TO TELL ME that "things happen for a reason," so I tried to tell myself that getting a very late start for my trip into Michigan's "thumb" area was only a minor annoyance, not a major catastrophe. But I was on a tight schedule—or so I kept telling myself. Little about the two days I spent exploring the thumb went as planned, but it was one of the best adventures of my trip around the state hunting ghost stories.

I started out getting on the road considerably later than I had planned—such is the way of things when there's a teenager to get off to school and she misses her bus. Instead of coffee and toast, my day started with "Mom, can you drive me to school?"

The delay worked out in my favor, however, because as soon as I arrived at my first stop, Castaways Food & Spirits in Lapeer, I realized that I had apparently misread the information on their website. I *thought* they opened at 11:00 in the morning. I must have missed a digit, because according to the sign on the door, they didn't open until 1:00 p.m. It was a very good thing I was there at 12:30, rather than bright and early at 11:00, as I had originally planned.

There were a few staff members on duty getting the place ready to open up, and one of them, a waitress named Kim, was kind enough to open the door and say "hello" when she saw me standing there looking in—and probably looking a little frazzled as well. It wasn't just the late start or the construction along the way; when my directions had me turning onto a dirt road, I started to wonder if I'd printed a map to the wrong place. Then again, what better place for a haunted building than at the bottom of a hill before a lake?

Kim was gracious about my early arrival. "We're not quite open yet, but if you want to come in and wait, you're welcome to have a seat. I was just finishing cleaning up."

I explained that I wasn't there for lunch, I was writing a book about haunted locations in Michigan and wondered if she could tell me anything about the restaurant's alleged ghostly activity.

"Oh, we have plenty of that," Kim said.

"I don't suppose you have a few minutes to talk to me about it?" I asked, hopefully.

She did, and she led me to a quiet table near the front of the dining room where we could talk. The restaurant hadn't looked like much from the outside, but I found the interior to be comfortable and the view of the lake was spectacular through the restaurant's huge windows. I could easily see why Nepessing Lake, which is one of the larger lakes in Lapeer County, was such a popular destination with fishers and boaters.

"What do you want to know about the place?" Kim asked me, as I drew my notebook out of my purse.

"Anything you want to tell me," I said. I explained that I was driving around the state, talking to folks and gathering their ghost stories, either firsthand accounts or anything customers or fellow employees might have reported.

"There's been a lot," she said. "Most of it seems to happen in the back." Kim nodded toward the back of the dining room. "I was cleaning back there one morning before we opened, and I heard this loud stomp, stomp, stomp above me, like someone was walking around on the roof or something." She demonstrated by slapping her palms against the tabletop, to emphasize that it wasn't a soft scuttling, but loud, distinct stomping. "It *wasn't* an animal," she insisted. "And I know there was no one on the roof. Now, we do have a crawl space between the ceiling and the roof, but no way it's big enough for a full-grown man to stand up in, let alone walk around."

Okay, I had to admit that might freak me out a little bit.

"That's the only thing that really happened to me, personally," she said. "But other people have said they get a weird feeling back there. And we've had a few paranormal groups come out to investigate the place. They came in with all their equipment, cameras and stuff, and I know they took a bunch of pictures that had those orbs in them."

Perhaps it was little wonder that Flint radio station WCRZ rated Castaways Food & Spirits as one of their top five haunted places near Flint, which is pretty impressive when you consider the other places that made the list (the Holly Hotel, Fenton Hotel, Flint's Capitol Theatre, and the River Rest and Sunset Hills Cemetery.) By comparison, the Castaways restaurant is very small and out-of-the-way.

But there's more going on at Castaways Food & Spirits than just Kim hearing footsteps on the roof when there couldn't have been anyone up there and the orb photos that were taken in the back room.

I did some more research on Castaways and discovered that some people claim to have heard voices whispering in the back of the dining room where Kim indicated most of the activity seemed to be centered, although she said there has been some activity in the lighthouse as well. One customer even reported seeing a woman leaning over the railing of the lighthouse, even though there was no way for someone to have gotten up there. Other people have said they felt "uneasy" in the back of the dining room and even in the restroom area, but Kim didn't think that whoever or whatever was haunting the place was malignant.

"You just hear weird noises once in a while. It's an old building and has its ghosts," she told me.

I said that that has pretty much been the consensus among people I've talked to who work in haunted places. Most people are comfortable with their spectral coinhabitants—and some places even make a pretty big deal out of being haunted. The Castaways' owners neither try to hide the fact that their restaurant is haunted, nor do they make a big deal out of it—although they do consider the name, Castaways Food & Spirits, to be somewhat tongue-in-cheek. For the most part, the ghosts are just there, occasionally clomping around on the roof, but not really bothering anybody and certainly not causing any harm.

Kim hazarded a guess as to the identity of the spirit who sometimes walks around on the roof. "There was a fireman who is supposed to have died in a fire, back when this place was the Nepessing Lake Hotel," she said. Kim took me over to one of the walls, where several old photos of the building were hanging, so I could see the pictorial history of the property for myself. "This is what it looked like back then—the building is something like a hundred years old," she added.

The building was clearly much larger in its younger years and looked like it must have had guest rooms in a second story that no longer exists.

"There was a fire at the old hotel, and the story goes that one of the firemen perished while trying to put it out. There's another story that the place was a brothel at one point too."

Kim walked me back to the front door; I thanked her for her time and let her get back to setting up for the day, then went outside and took a few photographs of the building before heading back up the dirt road and finding my way back to the highway.

While writing this chapter, I revisited the Castaway's website and discovered that their hours *are* listed as opening at 11:00 a.m. Monday through Saturday (on Sunday they open at noon). So I don't know if the late start on the day I visited was due to the fact that it was the week before Easter, or perhaps it was just that it was still fairly early in the season, but visitors might want to call ahead before venturing out to Lapeer.

CHAPTER 11

Time on Main Euro Café
RICHMOND

I LEFT LAPEER AND SET OFF for Richmond in search of a place I'd read about on a couple of paranormal researchers' websites. The name of the place was the Main Street Café. I had only the address and a few interesting stories to go on, but it seemed worth the trip and was only a little "out of the way."

My method for finding new places to investigate is relatively simple. I pick a destination—in this case, it was the city of Bay Port at the tip of the thumb. Bay Port is home to a reportedly very haunted Sweet Dreams Inn. I mapped my route and went searching for other allegedly haunted places between home and Bay Port by plugging "haunted places in . . ." into a search engine. I came up with a lot of commercial haunted houses, the kind you visit around Halloween, but I also came up with some interesting possibilities—and a few dead ends—that didn't show up in blanket searches for "haunted places in Michigan." Sometimes, you just have to be specific.

I arrived in Richmond and began cruising down Main Street, searching for my destination. After two passes through the few blocks that make up downtown Richmond, I was beginning to think I had hit one of those dead ends again. There was no Main Street Café anywhere in sight. But rather than give up, I decided to stop into the one café I had passed, a bright yellow building on the corner of Main and Park Streets, right in front of the famous town clock. The sign on the door read TIME ON MAIN EURO CAFÉ. Perhaps the Main Street Café had changed names since the articles I had read online were written. I parked around the back and went inside, hoping that I was in the right place—or that somebody could tell me where the right place was.

It was midafternoon and the cozy little café was empty except for a middle-aged man and woman who were behind the counter, cleaning up and taking care of some paperwork between shifts. They both looked up when I came in and greeted me with warm, welcoming smiles.

"What can we do for you?" the man asked me, in a friendly tone.

I explained that I was a little lost, that I was actually looking for the Main Street Café but couldn't find it. "I'm writing a book about haunted places in Michigan," I added. "And they came up in my research."

The woman nodded at me. "They used to be located just down the street," she said, "near the railroad tracks."

The words "used to be" did not bode well.

The woman went on to say that she had definitely heard of some odd things that used to happen there. In addition to the stories I'd read online, she said she had heard that people used to smell cigar smoke around the place, even though there was no one around smoking—sometimes when there was no one around at all.

Despite this new story, I felt a distinct pang of disappointment at the way she kept speaking of the Main Street Café in the past tense. It must have shown on my face, because she suggested that I go down to where they used to be and check it out. There was a construction company there now, and maybe the people who worked there had had the same allegedly ghostly encounters as the employees of the café.

Then she thought for a minute. "Or you could go next to the construction shop, to Crimson and Clover. I'll bet they could tell you some stories."

"Crimson and Clover?" I asked.

It turned out to be a florist shop. Deciding that something was better than nothing, I thanked the couple for their time and was getting ready to head out when the man—who had mostly been staying out of the conversation—came over and asked about the book I was writing.

"What got you interested in ghosts?" he wanted to know. "Do you have some kind of background in the paranormal?"

I'm always careful how I answer questions like that one. My job as a writer is to be as objective as possible, and I really don't have any kind of paranormal background, just an interest in things that can't necessarily be explained by science. I'm still a pretty big skeptic, however.

"When I was a little kid, I used to love *In Search of . . .* with Leonard Nemoy," I told him. It's true; it was one of my favorite shows, but admitting it immediately reveals my age. The original *In Search of . . .* was on in the 1970s.

The woman immediately smiled and told me that that used to be one of *her* favorite television shows, too. "There are just so many things that science hasn't explained yet," she said.

We finally got around to introductions, and I discovered that my hosts were owners Mimi and Philip Apollonio, and they were both interested in hearing more about some of the places I'd already visited and what kinds of stories people had told me. Since I didn't think either the construction company or florist shop were going to yield much—and because both Mimi and Philip had been so nice—I decided I had time to hang out for a while and chat. It wasn't long before Philip made me an espresso and the more we talked about other people's ghost stories, the more he and Mimi opened up about *their* shop and *their* ghost stories.

The building, which is now the Time on Main Euro Café, was once the home of Richmond's founding father, Erastus Beebe, who came to Michigan in 1835 with the dream of building a thriving community out of Michigan's wilderness. Wandering around the quiet, historic downtown area on the day I visited, I had to say Mr. Beebe succeeded. A major part of the city's early economic success was due, no doubt, to the railroad that came to town in 1859, when the Grand Trunk Railway Company laid tracks through town.

Mimi dug out some old news clippings and photocopies of the original property deed to show me some of the businesses and people who had owned the building before she and Philip took it over and turned it into a café. After Erastus Beebe moved out, the house went through several owners and was the home of several kinds of businesses, including a local newspaper and a blacksmith's shop.

"We were cleaning up when we first came here," Philip told me, "and found some old equipment and other things from when it was a blacksmith's. We found all kinds of stuff."

They also discovered that their shop might be haunted.

"Some of it might be nothing," Philip cautioned me. "Like sometimes the blender will go on all by itself, but I don't know if that's a spirit or what." Philip seemed pretty cautious about blaming the occasional odd occurrence on ghosts, but he did agree that there were some odd things that had happened in the café.

That's when Mimi jumped in to tell me how one night Philip had come home from working late in the office, which is on the second floor of the café. "He was really shaken up," she said. "He told me that all of a sudden the office got really cold."

The sudden chill was unexplainable, according to Philip.

There have been other unusual incidences at the café as well. Mimi told me that a number of people, including her and Philip as well as her sister and father, have heard people walking around on the hardwood floors, even when no one else should have been in the building.

"My sister looked right at Philip and said 'Someone's here, go look and see who it is,'" said Mimi.

"There wasn't anybody," Philip told me. "The place was empty except for us."

Customers have seen and heard things too. Mimi told me about one woman in particular who insisted that someone had come in the front door. "She said it was a man wearing a hat." But there wasn't any man with a hat in the restaurant. Sometime after that, Philip and Mimi put bells on the front door—and every once in a while someone still says they see a phantom customer come in, even though the door doesn't open and the bells don't jingle.

I finished my espresso and thanked Mimi and Philip for their warm hospitality. Before I took my leave, Mimi suggested that in addition to going by the florist's shop, I should head up the road into Memphis. There was a bar there I had to see. She couldn't remember the name, but she was certain I couldn't miss it. "It's a big white building, right off the main road. Go in and talk to Mike—tell him Phil and I sent you. He's been in here a few times telling us about what goes on at his place and . . . it's pretty interesting."

What had started out as apparently a dead end had turned into an incredible afternoon. Not only were Mimi and Philip wonderful hosts, but I left their café with two solid leads—and all because I stopped to talk to them.

Boomers Tavern
MEMPHIS

FOLLOWING MY SECOND LEAD from Mimi and Philip at the Time on Main Café in Richmond, I headed back up M-19 (Main Street/Memphis Ridge Road) to the tiny little town of Memphis, Michigan, to look for a man named Mike. Although Mimi hadn't been able to remember the name of Mike's bar, her assessment that I "wouldn't be able to miss it" was completely accurate, and within ten minutes I was parked across the street from Boomers Tavern. Standing almost exactly at the center of downtown Memphis at the corner of Bordman Road and M-19, the big, white building looked as if it might have at one time been someone's home, or perhaps a boarding house. I parked across the street and ventured over.

I have to admit I felt a bit of trepidation as I approached; the building looked old. Really old. But Mimi and Philip hadn't steered me wrong so far, so I was willing to give it a shot and walked up the front porch to try one of the doors.

"Can I help you?" called a voice.

I glanced down to see a man wearing a shirt with the name Mikey written across the pocket. I suspected that he was who I was looking for, but asked anyway.

"Hi," I greeted him with a smile. "Mimi and Philip from the café in Richmond said I should come by. They said to ask for Mike."

About then someone driving down Bordman slowed and called "Hey Mike!" out the window of his truck.

Mike turned and waved to the driver, then looked back at me with an amused smile. "I'm Mike," he told me, needlessly. "What can I do for you?"

I introduced myself and explained, "I'm writing a book about haunted places in Michigan—" I didn't get any further than that, however, before he told me that I had *definitely* come to the right place if I wanted haunted.

"What do you want to know?" he asked.

Well, that was easy! I explained that I was traveling around the state visiting reputedly haunted locations, the kinds of places readers would be able to visit for themselves, and that Mimi and Philip suggested I come up to Memphis. "I'm not trying to prove or disprove anything," I cautioned. "I'm just listening to people's stories and writing them down so my readers can judge for themselves."

He laughed. "Well, I've got a few ghost stories for you, that's for sure. We've had a couple of paranormal groups come out here to investigate the place too. This is probably the oldest building in Memphis," he added. "It was originally a hotel—"

Someone else driving by called out to Mike to say hello and

ask about an event going on at the tavern later that night. They talked for a couple of seconds, and then Mike turned back to me with an apologetic smile. "Sorry about that."

"I guess your customers aren't scared by the ghosts," I remarked.

"Nah, not really. Where was I?"

I reminded him that he was telling me about the history of the place. It was a subject Mike had researched diligently with the help of the Memphis Historical Society—admittedly a fairly small group, he added, but he was proud to be a part of it.

The building that is now Boomers Tavern was constructed in 1855 and was originally a stagecoach stop. During the early 1900s, it became The National Hotel, and a pretty big deal, according to Mike, who told me that it used to be a three-story building rather than the two-story structure that stands there today. I could only imagine that it must have been a big place in its day, with the main floor as a dining area, ten guest bedrooms on the second floor, and a ballroom on the third. Unfortunately, in 1962 a fire destroyed the third story. While the guest rooms remain intact, it has been decades since the place was used as a hotel. "Although the people we bought it from in 2007 lived up on the second floor," he added.

He went on to say that the previous owner never had any unusual experiences in the building—but he described the former owner as an older fellow, so maybe he just didn't notice.

Given some of the things Mike told me he heard about the building before he bought it, I had to wonder how anyone wouldn't notice it—assuming the rumors were true.

"People used to claim to see 'guests' walking around upstairs or peering out of the windows on the second floor when no one was up there," Mike told me. He also said that there have been two confirmed deaths on the property, one a murder, the other someone who died of natural causes. "That was about 20 years ago and happened in one of the corner bedrooms." He pointed up to one of the windows to indicate which room.

But Mike didn't necessarily believe in the rumors himself, at least not until a series of unexplainable incidents in the bar— glasses sliding down the bar or falling off shelves and unlocked doors mysteriously locking all by themselves—made Mike begin to suspect there might be something to the ghost stories after all. Some of his bartenders, and even a few customers, also told him that every once in a while they heard what sounded like a baby crying in the bar area, but when they looked around they could see no children in the bar.

Then one day, Mike got a visit from a couple of members of ESP Michigan, a group of professional paranormal investigators who operate out of Macomb County. Like me, the members of ESP Michigan had heard about Boomers while they were in the area investigating other places and decided to check out the tavern. They talked for a while, and Mike decided to let them investigate.

"They were completely professional," he told me. "They set up their equipment in one of the upstairs bedrooms and in the bathroom." Like most old inns, there was only one bathroom upstairs, which was shared by all of the guests. He said the bathroom upstairs was one of the most active rooms in the building when it came to paranormal phenomena. "Would you like a tour of the upstairs?" Mike asked.

I was more than happy to accept, even though he warned me that upstairs wasn't in the best state. For years, it hadn't been used for anything but storage.

"Watch your step," he cautioned as we climbed the narrow back stairs off the tavern's kitchen.

Once upstairs, he showed me the communal bathroom and pointed out the room that still seems to become locked "all by itself." The room used to belong to the former owner's mother, he told me.

"We usually leave the keys in the door," he said. "It's just easier that way."

The story goes that shortly after Mike and his wife bought the building, they noticed that no matter how many times they unlocked it, they would always find a certain door locked again the next time they came up to get something or put something away.

There was another room that Mike wanted me to see too. "When the ghosthunters were here, they told me that they discovered this room used to be a nursery," he explained. "What's interesting about that is that another lady who claimed to be psychic told me the same thing."

It certainly was interesting to hear that two people who had never spoken to each other both said the room upstairs had been a nursery, but, "Did either of them know the story about your staff hearing a baby crying?" I asked.

Mike said that as far as he knew, they hadn't. He told me that the ghosthunters had taken a number of photographs with orbs in them, particularly over one door. He also suggested that I check out their website, where they had posted some of the footage from their investigation. I found it on ESP Michigan's Facebook page. The footage isn't very conclusive, but there is one place in the clip where I could see a shadow pass across the camera. Supposedly, none of the team members walked in front of any of their lights; they were all standing more or less still when the shadow passed in front of the door.

Mike took me downstairs to show me some books and a calendar he had from the historical society. It was filled with old photographs of the town, including several of the bar from when it was a stagecoach stop and a three-story hotel. Mike made photocopies of some of the material for me.

He concluded my visit with one last story, as he pointed out the jukebox. "It's basically like satellite radio," he explained. "You can get just about any song you want, not like the old jukeboxes that had records in them."

I laughed—I'm just old enough to remember those.

"It was the night the ghosthunters were here," he went on. "I had a customer who was trying to get a song to play—I don't remember which one now, just that no matter what we did, it wouldn't play. I gave him his money back and it was no big deal. But that night, after we closed up—and after we turned the jukebox *off*—it suddenly turned back on again and the song the customer had been trying to play came on. There's no reason for it to have done that—other customers had played other songs after that, so it's not like it got stuck or something."

I thanked Mike for his hospitality, and then it was time for me to hit the road again.

Spotlight On: EVP
(Electronic Voice Phenomena)

If you visit any paranormal investigator's website, you will likely find clips of EVP recordings that were captured during the course of their investigations. I have to confess, most of the EVP recordings I've listened to sound like either white noise or garbled nonsense. The human mind is very susceptible to suggestion. Just like we often see what we want to see, we also frequently hear what we want to hear. But every once in a while I run across an EVP recording that makes me doubt my own skepticism, because it sounds so clear and the words spoken are so distinct. Of course, this could be because the recording device is picking up a radio station or even CB (citizens band radio) chatter—except that quite frequently the recorded voices are responding to questions or even calling investigators by name. What is interesting about these recordings is that the ghostly responses can only be heard on the tape; they aren't detectable by human ears otherwise.

For as long as there have been audio recording devices, there have been people attempting to record the voices of the dead. Even Thomas Edison is said to have attempted to make contact with the spirit world in the 1890s—he wasn't successful. The first known EVP recording wasn't captured until 1938; the recording was made with a phonograph (an early record player).

But it was Friedrich Jergenson (1903–1987) who truly pioneered the study of electronic voice phenomena. The story says that he was recording bird songs and when he played the recording back, he realized there were human voices in the background. Jergenson didn't recall having heard any people where he was recording. His curiosity aroused, he began making "recordings of nothing," simply setting up his equipment in a quiet places, with no other people around to see what he could capture on tape. Ultimately, he claimed to have recorded the voice of his own long-dead mother and came to believe that somehow he was recording voices from beyond the grave. Many researchers have followed after Jergenson, attempting to both prove and disprove his theories.

Almost any recording device can be used to record EVPs; although these days, digital recorders are probably the most popular. They're small, inexpensive, and have greater recording times than audiocassettes. The important thing is to have a sensitive microphone, because often ghostly voices caught on tape are speaking in hushed whispers. Many paranormal investigators suggest using an external microphone rather than relying on the microphone built into your recorder.

The technique most often employed by investigators is to begin by asking any ghosts in the area to talk to you. You might then ask a series of questions, such as "what is your name?" "where are you from?" and "why are you here?" Pause after each question to give the spirits the opportunity to respond. When you're done, you can play back the recording to see if you've captured anything that sounds like an answer. Experts say the best EVP recordings are the ones that sound like real human voices.

Another method of gathering audio evidence of supernatural activity is to do like I did at the Blue Pelican Inn and simply leave your recorder on all night—but that can make for some very boring listening the next day!

CHAPTER 13

Forester Township Cemetery
FORESTER

I HAD BEEN RELUCTANT TO WRITE about cemeteries, even though it's where one would think looking for ghost stories would be the easiest. But part of my job—in fact the part I love the most—in writing this book is talking to people. Hearing their ghost stories. It's hard to do that in a cemetery. Lighthouses, restaurants, and theaters all have employees I can talk to. With a cemetery, it is a lot harder to find an employee on duty. Besides, a good deal of the activity that allegedly takes place at cemeteries happens after dark, which in most cases is when cemeteries are closed to the public.

But when I left Mimi and Philip Apollonio at the Time on Main Café, I went down to the Crimson and Clover florist shop.

I explained to the gal behind the counter that I had been sent down because there was a chance she or her coworkers had experienced some of the same unusual goings on that the employees of the Main Street Café used to, before the business was sold.

She had . . . but she wasn't comfortable talking about it in any detail; I should really ask her boss but she was off for the weekend. We exchanged business cards, and we talked for a couple of minutes, because, once again, I had run into someone who was interested in the project I was working on.

"Do you know the story of Minnie Quay?" she asked me.

No, I hadn't heard it, but that was probably because I wasn't really investigating people; I was looking into haunted places. Of course, that didn't mean I wasn't eager to hear what the gal in the florist shop had to tell me. Some of the best leads can be garnered just by talking to people, as Mimi and Philip had so recently proven to me.

"Me and my friends visit Minnie Quay's grave every time we drive out to Caseville," the young lady at the florist shop told me. "A lot of people do. You're supposed to go and leave something for her, like a token, because her story is so sad. She was in love with a sailor who died in a shipwreck and it broke her heart so much that she walked into Lake Huron and drowned. Lots of people have seen her ghost walking along the shore," she added.

That story sparked my interest enough that after I checked into a motel for the night, I booted up my laptop and did some digging. It wasn't long before I was figuring out the best way to work the Forester Township Cemetery into my trip.

Forester is an unincorporated township on Lake Huron's coast, located about 60 miles north of Port Huron. And it is truly little more than a dot on the map. With a population of barely over a thousand people spread out over 25 square miles (very little of it built up in any significant way), the first thing I discovered when I arrived at Forester Township Cemetery is that the address I found online for the cemetery does not correspond with its actual location. Fortunately, it wasn't off by more than a few hundred feet, and the cemetery itself wasn't difficult to find, so even though my GPS told me to keep driving, I turned into the little graveyard anyway. Once I parked, the search for the Quay family plot began. I was more than grateful that the Forester Township Cemetery wasn't especially large. The headstone I eventually found, marked Quay/Shaw, seemed to be a different stone from the one I had seen a photo of online—but there was plenty of evidence of visitors leaving tokens for Minnie. I figured that even if I didn't have the "right" Quay grave site, I at least was at one that was visited by people who had wished to pay their respects to the lovelorn young woman.

The Quay/Shaw headstone I visited is off the southern road into the cemetery, about halfway to the back. The headstone faces the back of the cemetery, perhaps intentionally, as the cemetery overlooks Lake Huron. Later, I found out that "Shaw" is the name of the last descendants of the Quay family, so it could be that I had been in the right place after all and that the headstone had simply been updated.

Unlike a lot of other urban legends, especially those attached to cemeteries—and *especially* those you find online—the facts of Minnie Quay's story are true. She was born in 1861 and lived in Forester with her parents, Mary Ann and James, and a younger brother. Although Forester doesn't look like much now, when the Quay family was living, it was, like so many other little towns in Michigan, a city booming with industry and commerce. As a result, freighters and their crews were frequently coming and going through town. Unfortunately, sailors have never enjoyed a very good reputation, and when Minnie Quay, a young woman of 15 or 16 (accounts vary) fell in love with one, her parents were not happy. No information

Gifts left by visitors to the Quay/Shaw tombstone at Forester Cemetery.

seems to be recorded about the young man, so it is impossible to say whether or not his intentions were noble or, as the Quays no doubt feared, he had a girl in every port. All that is known is that James and Mary Ann forbid their daughter to continue the affair. When Minnie refused to break it off, her parents forcibly moved the girl out of her own room into a small bedroom adjacent to their own, probably originally a nursery. The next time Minnie's young sailor came into town, James and Mary Ann locked their daughter in that room and refused to let her out until he was gone.

In early spring of 1876, word reached Minnie that the ship her lover had been on was caught in a storm on the lake and sank. All hands on board were drowned. Minnie's grief was doubled because not only was her lover dead, but her parents had prevented her from seeing him the last time he was in town. Had she been allowed to see him, she would at least have been able to say goodbye before what would be his last voyage.

On May 26, 1876, Minnie's parents left her in charge of her younger brother while they went out to run errands. Shortly after James and Mary Ann left the house, Minnie put her brother down for a nap and walked down to the lake, wearing a white gown, according to eyewitnesses. She walked to Forester Pier, just past the Tanner House hotel where bystanders watched in shock and horror as she jumped to her death off the end of the pier into Lake Huron.

Her restless spirit is said to wander along the shore near the remains of Forester Pier at night, and many people claim to have seen her, including several people I talked to when I stopped for gas just outside of town. The stories were all pretty much the same: someone walking along the beach near Forester Pier at night would spot a figure off in the distance and assume it was someone else out for a stroll until they looked back and the other person wasn't there anymore. Locals believe that Minnie was never reunited with her sailor, even in death, which is why she still haunts the beach where she drowned. Her ghost has also allegedly been spotted around the old Tanner House hotel, which still stands and is located at the corner of M-25 and Forester Road.

Minnie's story was so moving to talented Michigander Jory Brown that he wrote a folk ballad entitled "The Ghost of Minnie Quay." His wife, Karen, put together the video, which can be found on Youtube.

Whether you believe in ghosts or not, Minnie Quay's story is certainly a tragic one.

CHAPTER 14

Sweet Dreams Inn Victorian Bed & Breakfast

BAY PORT

OWNED AND OPERATED by the Chaperon family, the Sweet Dreams Inn is a beautiful 122-year-old Victorian mansion in Bay Port, at the very tip of Michigan's "thumb." Like most bed-and-breakfasts, the Sweet Dreams Inn is the Chaperon's family home as well as their business, and I was grateful to Julia Chaperon for taking some time out of her hectic schedule to talk to me when I called on her the week before Easter. Julia was in the middle of preparing for the arrival of family members from Greece but still took the time to let me come out and have a look around.

Built in 1890, the Sweet Dreams Inn overlooks Wild Fowl Bay on Lake Huron; nearby cities include Caseville and Port Austin, both popular destinations for visitors interested in exploring Michigan's rich history and culture. There are numerous small museums, lighthouses, antiques shops, and historical sites to explore nearby, as well as beautiful beaches, marinas, golf courses, and hiking trails. The Sweet Dreams Inn is one of the few bed-and-breakfasts I've visited over the years where children are welcome (in their third-floor suite only)—although the owners state one caveat on their website: the inn is haunted. Refunds are not issued to guests too frightened by things going bump in the night to remain on the premises.

When I spoke to Julia, I asked her about her no-refunds policy. "Has it really been that big of a problem?"

"Oh, yes," she assured me. "It wasn't that we started out to operate as a haunted hotel; that was *never* my intention. But the ghosts are here, and they make their presence known. I would have guests knocking on my bedroom door in the middle of the night, waking me up, because they were too scared to stay and wanted a refund. I finally had to put it on our website. We're haunted. If you can't handle that, you should stay somewhere else."

I wondered if that had hurt business any.

Julia didn't think so. "Once people started putting stuff on websites like Shadowlands, talking about how haunted we are, we started getting guests who wanted to come out and stay here *because* we're so haunted. We've had tons of articles written about us in local papers and magazines, and I've gotten calls from radio stations wanting to know more about our ghosts. A couple of years ago TV 25, out of Flint, came out and did a huge two-part feature on the inn," she added.

Julia went on to tell me that one of the reporters was so freaked out by what had happened while the crew was out at the inn during the day that he refused to come back at night, for the second part of the feature.

"We were inside the house," Julia explained, "and we kept hearing this knocking sound on the exterior walls, like someone was outside pounding on them. We sent someone outside to see if maybe it was a woodpecker or something—but nothing was there. We kept on hearing it inside, even while he was walking around outside, trying to figure out what was making the noise."

So just who are the ghostly residents of the Sweet Dreams Inn?

Julia said she thought they were members of the Wallace family. "William H. Wallace owned this house," she said. "He used to own most of the land around Bay Port."

Looking at the house, I wasn't surprised that William Wallace was a wealthy man in his day. In addition to all the usual amenities of a Victorian-era home, the Wallace house once featured a third-floor ballroom with vaulted ceilings that the family used for entertaining, something they did a lot of, according to local historians.

The third floor has since been converted into a large bedroom that sleeps up to six guests and, like the rest of the house, it seems to be quite haunted. Guests have reported being touched or poked while on the third floor, and photographs taken up there often show a "black mass in the corners." Julia also told me that a number of people have reported seeing a young woman peering out of the third-floor windows, even though there was no one in the house at the time. She suspects that it might be the spirit of Ora Wallace, daughter of William Wallace and his second wife, Francis. Julia described Ora to me as a "wild child."

"The story is that she used to climb out of her bedroom and down the side of the house, maybe on the gutter or something," said Julia, "to go into town where she drank and caroused with all the boys. Eventually her mother locked her in a long closet upstairs. Maybe that's why she haunts the third floor."

Despite all that, it isn't the third floor that's the most haunted, according to Julia. It's the Peacock Room, on the second floor of the house. "We used to call it the Rose Room," she told me, "but changed it a while back because we had another room with a similar name."

Regardless of what it's called, I wasn't sure it was a room *I* would want to stay in after Julia got done telling me about everything that went on up there.

"We're pretty sure that's the room where William Wallace's first wife, Elizabeth, passed away," she began. "So that's probably why he always paces around up there so much."

I wondered how often she heard him, and she explained that when Wallace got into "one of his moods," he'd go at it every night for a week or more. "Sometimes he's up there pacing for 30 or 40 minutes," she said.

After we spoke, Julia asked Scott Morgan, the head of the South East Michigan Paranormal Society (SEMPS), to send me a video clip from the last investigation his team did at the Sweet Dreams Inn. There was a spot on the clip where it truly did sound as if someone was walking back and forth in the bedroom—but the only person visible in the room was Scott, sitting on the bed.

Julia told me that it was Scott and his team who first identified the ghost in the room as William Wallace, simply by asking him "who are you?"

Julia said they heard the reply on the tape later: *William Wallace.*

In addition to having paranormal investigators come to the house, Julia has had a number of psychics out as well.

"I had one lady call me and ask for 'the Mrs.' Room.' I knew she must mean the Peacock Room, so that's the room I booked her into. When she arrived, she took me through my own house and told things about it she had no way of knowing. It was really creepy. She was able to tell me which rooms had belonged to which of the Wallace kids, and when we got to the Peacock Room, she said, 'This is the room where Elizabeth Wallace died.'"

Other spirits allegedly haunt the room where Elizabeth Wallace died. Julia told me that numerous guests have reported childlike ghosts "playing" in the room all the time. She thought that was probably because Elizabeth's five children would visit her in her sickbed.

"The kids put their little hands into guests' hands in that room," said Julia. "I had one guest who told me he laid his wallet on the desk, and the kids kept making it spin around like they were playing with it." She said that particular family has been back many times over the years. They told her they travel quite a bit and that the Sweet Dreams Inn is "one of the most haunted places they've ever stayed."

Little surprise: Elizabeth Wallace wasn't the only family member to die on the premises. Julia told me she later discovered that William's son Billy also died in the house.

She went on to tell me about an experience one of her friends had in the Peacock Room. "I had some girlfriends up for a girls' weekend. The first night, they all stayed on the third floor, but the second night my one friend wanted to stay in the Peacock Room. She didn't believe all the stuff I'd told her went on here, so she wanted to see for herself whether it was for real or not. I said sure, and she moved her stuff downstairs. What I didn't know at the time was that she'd gone to the store and bought a bunch of little toy cars. She left them around the room—I guess to see if the ghost kids would play with them. The next morning, my friend told me that she woke up with one of the cars in her hand. She finally believed me that the place is haunted."

That would be pretty convincing, all right.

"So what's it like living in such a haunted house?" I asked.

"It's been interesting," she answered. "I didn't live here full-time when I first bought the house, about ten years ago. I still had a place in the city and just came up on the weekends. Usually, I'd arrive on Friday night, and guests wouldn't come in until Saturday. One Friday night I was sitting watching television in the parlor, and suddenly my dog starts barking in the next room. I went to see what in the world he could be so riled up about, and he was staring up at one of the wall sconces." The wall sconces she was talking about all had pull-cords to turn them on and off. The cord of the sconce her dog was barking at was swinging back and forth so hard, Julia said, it was hitting the wall. There was no way it could have been caused by a draft. "You'd have to hit it pretty hard to get it to smack against the wall like that," she added emphatically.

Julia had a routine, she told me, for closing up the house at the end of the weekend. She would go through and clean everything up, turn off all but one light, turn down the thermostat, and lock up for the week. But invariably she would arrive on Friday to find the door still locked, but the lights on and the heat turned up as high as it would go. Unsettled, she called the police, who refused to believe that something strange was going on. "They said that I was 'from the city and didn't know what I was talking about.' They were sure I was either making the whole thing up or had simply forgotten to turn the lights off before I left."

There would be other times when Julia was sitting in the living room and could hear "someone running up and down the stairs." She explained to me that there were two staircases leading from the first floor to the second, and one staircase leading from the second floor to the third. There was also only one set of stairs leading from the ground floor into the basement.

"So, I'd be sitting down here in the parlor, and I would hear footsteps running down the stairs from the third floor to the second floor, down the back hall, and then down the back stairs, into the kitchen. Then the door to the basement would slam, and I'd hear footsteps running down into the basement. Or sometimes I'd heard footsteps on the back landing and hear the back door slam. I really thought someone must have a key to my house or something. I put a bell on the back door—and I'd hear that ring as the door slammed. But every time I got up and looked, no one was there."

There were other times when Julia said she would hear the fan in one of the bathrooms go on, because "someone" had turned the light on. No one else was home, of course. "Then a few minutes later, I'd hear the fan in another bathroom go on. Sometimes I have to tell them to knock it off. Usually they listen."

Then she told me another story: "We have well water," she began, "so when I have guests staying for the whole weekend, I'll put a gallon of bottled water in their rooms. A lot of people don't like well water. When the doors slamming gets to be too much, guests tell me that they put the gallon jug in front of the door, to keep it shut. The ghosts push the doors open, anyway."

Obviously, Julia and her family aren't afraid of living in a haunted house, but what I wondered was whether the previous owners warned her that the house came with ghostly residents.

"To this day, they deny that it's haunted," she told me. She said the previous owners were an older couple, so maybe they just didn't hear all the clomping around upstairs or the footsteps running up and down the stairs—or maybe the ghosts just weren't active for them. "The couple who owned the house before me did a lot of renovating," Julia explained. "Maybe that made the spirits more active, I don't know."

I wasn't very convinced about that, especially after Julia told me that her neighbors had apparently known the place was haunted all along, but they just neglected to mention any of the odd goings on to her.

"My neighbors were never very friendly to me," Julia explained. "I didn't know why. It was only later that I figured it out."

She explained that on one of their visits, the members of the South East Michigan Paranormal Society had gone into town to get a bite to eat, and some of the locals told them that they had "always known the Wallace house was haunted, but we don't want anything to do with it."

"Basically, I think they were scared of the place," said Julia.

I thanked her for her time again and headed off on my trek home—it was getting late and I had a long drive ahead of me, but I wasn't sure I wanted to ask if she had a room I could rent for the night. . . .

Spotlight On: Richmond's Main Street Café

I initially travelled to Richmond, near the base of Michigan's thumb area, looking for the Main Street Café, which had come up in my research as being haunted. After driving up and down Main Street a couple of times, I stopped into the only café I could find, Time on Main Street, where owners Mimi and Philip told me that the Main Street Café "used to be just down the street, right next to the railroad tracks." It wasn't there any more, however.

Even so, Mimi was able to confirm that the Main Street Café had indeed been haunted. She had heard several stories about how staff and customers would smell cigar or possibly pipe smoke from time to time, even when no one was around.

I found out later that former owners Kathy and Bernie Osebold had reported finding an indentation on the edge of the bed in the apartment upstairs, as if someone had been sitting there. The phantom lodger also apparently would knock things off the café's shelves.

When I walked down to the site of the former café, I found the Crimson and Clover florist shop. Although the young lady behind the counter wasn't comfortable getting into too many details with me, I got the impression that even though the café was no longer there, Earl, the café's resident specter, might still be.

The building most likely dates back to the turn of the 20th century, and most people believe that Earl was probably the original owner. Other than that, no one seemed to know very much about him, even though he was alleged to have manifested fully in front of the café's staff, as a man wearing a red plaid shirt and blue jeans. The story goes that paranormal activity dramatically increased just before there was a problem at the café, usually involving the electricity, wiring, or electrical equipment. The staff learned to keep an eye out for potential problems whenever Earl made his presence known. Most people suspected that whoever he really was in life, he was continuing to keep an eye on the place after death.

There is little documentation available about the building's history, or what it might have been before it was the Main Street Café. I was also unable to dig up much information about why the café closed, only that it shut its doors for the final time after 2010.

Crimson and Clover is actually the building next door, a construction company occupies the former café's location—however, they were closed at the time I stopped in.

Western Michigan

Allegan
Grill House Restaurant
Regent Theatre

Grand Haven
Dee-Lite Bar & Grill
Kirby House

Kalamazoo
Henderson Castle

Marshall
The National House Inn

Plainwell
Sam's Joint

Portage
Stuart Manor

CHAPTER 15

Henderson Castle
KALAMAZOO

ALTHOUGH I WAS HEADED TO KALAMAZOO on a completely unrelated errand, I couldn't resist the urge to type "haunted places in Kalamazoo" into my favorite Internet search engine the night before I left. The first place to come up was Henderson Castle. As soon as I saw a picture of the place, I knew I wanted to visit! I didn't even know exactly what the castle was, I just knew it was open to the public and spectacularly beautiful. I'm a huge fan of Victorian architecture— I love old buildings in general, but Victorian-era houses are my favorite. The next question, of course, was "is it really haunted?" Experience has taught me that you can't believe everything you read online.

I did a little more digging and came up with an MLive.com news article confirming that there really were reports of ghostly activity at Henderson Castle and that the building had been visited by at least one paranormal investigation team, the Southern Michigan ParaNormals. They've been out to Henderson Castle several times over the past few years and have collected a good bit of evidence, mostly in the form of EVPs (electronic voice phenomena) and personal experiences, to support the claims that the ghosts of Mr. and Mrs. Frank Henderson, who built the castle in 1895, are still "in residence" in their former home.

There are several other spirits who seem to haunt the castle, including several children, probably little girls. They have been heard by both staff and guests, laughing in the halls—or so the story goes.

The castle—and, truly, Henderson Castle deserves the name "castle"—was originally a private home. But more than building his dream home, Frank Henderson had a hand in shaping the entire subdivision in which his castle resides. Sadly, however, Mr. Henderson only got to live in his dream house for four years. He passed away in 1899 and was buried in the cemetery across the street. His grave is on a hill, overlooking the castle. His wife, Mary, remained in their home for another nine years before moving away. The castle changed hands several times over the next few years, with each owner making his or her own changes.

Henderson Castle is reported to have cost $72,000 when it was built over a hundred years ago. There are 25 rooms, including seven baths, a sauna, and a ballroom on the third floor. Supposedly, a number of "secret passageways" are hidden throughout the house. I suspected as I was reading the articles that these were really just back halls intended for servants' use and not really secret passageways at all. We sometimes forget that a hundred years ago servants weren't supposed to be seen by their "betters."

A much later addition to the castle was a rooftop hot tub, which seems in keeping with Henderson's goal of building a home that, according to the castle's website, "exemplified the most expensive tastes of the time."

In the 1920s, the carriage house was converted into a garage, but that has since been turned into a separate residence. Later, in 1945, the main house was divided into apartments—and it must have been a magnificent place to live. Eventually, the castle became a part of Kalamazoo College but then was sold back into private ownership when Dr. Jess Walker purchased it in 1975. Dr. Walker began the arduous task of restoring the property; the task was taken over in 1981 by Fred Royce, who continued the job of restoring the castle and eventually turned it into a bed-and-breakfast. I was more than pleasantly surprised to discover that the room rates for an overnight stay at Henderson Castle are competitive with other bed-and-breakfasts (about the same as a three- or four-star hotel)—but I was really only planning a day trip. Maybe next time I have to head up that way, I'll stay overnight.

I printed my directions and finished getting my gear together for my road trip to Kalamazoo. I made sure I had fresh batteries for my camera—and a set of extras. After my visit to the Baldwin Theatre, I had learned my lesson. I bought an extra set of AAs to toss into my bag in case any mischievous ghosts (or my teenager) decided to get hold of my camera and drain the batteries. Once I had everything set, it was off to bed early; I wanted to get up and on the road early to avoid morning rush hour.

Kalamazoo proved to be about a three-hour drive from my metro-Detroit home—MapQuest had insisted it would only take *two* hours. They took me on four highways where I normally would have only taken two, I-75 and I-94. Lesson learned: next time I'll read over the directions *before* hitting the road. It was probably a good thing I'd left my husband at home that day. He no

Stained glass window in front of which a guest took a picture of Mr. Henderson's ghost.

doubt would have laughed at me—and he really doesn't have my passion for old houses or ghost stories.

It was a gorgeous day for a drive. I had the windows rolled down and the music turned up. I was excited about the trip in part because I hadn't been to Kalamazoo since I was in high school. In my senior year, we took a fieldtrip to Western Michigan University for a marching band competition. Needless to say, being there with 60 classmates and half a dozen chaperones, I didn't see much of the city, but I remember wishing I'd had more time for sightseeing. So I was looking forward to playing tourist, albeit tourist on a mission. In addition to Henderson Castle, there were three other places I wanted to visit. This time around, I hadn't made any appointments; I was just dropping in and hoping for the best.

Over the past few months I'd discovered that there wasn't any real secret to getting people to talk to me about their ghost stories, other than simply asking nicely. Some people have been amenable to being interviewed and happy to show me around, while employees at other venues are more reluctant. Only two, so far, have flat out asked me not to even mention their property at all. A couple of the places I've visited have required more than one trip to talk to the resident "expert" on the venue's ghosts, but I've had about the same success just "dropping in" as I've had when I'd tried to make an appointment. So as soon as I finished up my other errands, I headed to Kalamazoo's west side and Henderson Castle.

Kalamazoo's roads are a bit on the twisty side, but I only got lost once—Academe Street isn't clearly labeled on one side of the road. Once I found it, however, it was only a couple more turns before I discovered that pictures truly do not do Henderson Castle justice. Not only did it sit atop a very high hill, just like a real castle, but it was *so* much bigger in person than it looked online! For the first time since I'd started working on this project, I felt a little intimidated as I walked toward the front steps and up onto the huge, wrap-around porch. Was my slip showing? Was my hair still neat in its braid, or had a million little wisps flown loose like always?

Finding the front door open, I stepped quietly inside and found myself surrounded by polished wood, white marble, and gleaming brass. Classical music filled the foyer, and off to my left I saw the dining room. The tables were set with black cloths; it looked very regal.

No one seemed to be around to greet me, so I ventured further inside. Bed-and-breakfast inns are often also the proprietors' homes, and while most B & B owners welcome guests, they also have a business to run.

Finally, I spied an open door and a man in a chef's coat and jeans working at his computer. His back was to me, so I announced myself by saying, "Good morning."

He turned and greeted me with a welcoming smile. "Good morning, how are you today?"

Bolstered by the warmth of the chef's "hello," I held out my hand and introduced myself, hoping that even if the management of Henderson Castle didn't want their inn to end up in a book about ghosts, they might at least let me look around the grounds. I'm sure I sounded nervous as I explained the reason for my visit, but he just kept smiling. When I stopped to take a breath, he asked a few questions, and said that he was François. I realized he must be the owner, François Moyet, who had taken over Henderson Castle in August of 2011. He was also willing to give me a few minutes of his time.

"This place is . . . I'm not sure if I would say *haunted,*" François began, a little bit cautiously, "but we seem to have some interesting positive activity going on." He stressed that whatever was in the castle, it was definitely a benevolent entity that was looking out for him and his staff. "Most people say it's Mr. Henderson," he told me. "He wanted to be buried in the cemetery across the street. He's on the hill, so he can still see his house."

I suppose if I'd built my dream house and only gotten to live in it for a few years, I might want to keep an eye on it from the afterlife too.

François went on, "Personally, the only thing I really witnessed here . . . well, let me show you." He led the way toward the dining room. The room is lit by wall sconces—all electric, of course, but otherwise what you'd expect to see in a Victorian home (Victorians would have used gas to fuel their lights). François explained that although the lights each had individual on-off switches, they were all wired to a main switch at the doorway. That way, all he or someone else had to do was flip one switch to light up the entire room.

"It was the night of Halloween," he explained, "and I came in to turn the lights on. I flipped the switch, and nothing happened. At first I thought maybe we blew a fuse, but the fuses were all okay. So I came back up and walked over to the light." He walked me over to demonstrate—the switches on the sconces

themselves are tiny knobs that look more decorative than func-
tional. "I tried the switch. The light came on. If it had just been
one, I might have not thought anything of it, but every single
sconce was turned off at the switch, at the light itself." He felt
certain that no member of his staff or any of the guests were
responsible.

"I've felt some activity," he added, "whenever I've brought in
new furniture."

All of the furnishings in the castle appeared to be antiques,
and I remembered what both Lynn Hay and Patricia Kennedy
had told me, when I visited their shops in Holly: spirits seem to
become attached to things that belonged to them in life, especially dolls, mirrors, and larger items, like furniture. François
speculated that perhaps if any spirits had been attached to the
antiques he brought, those "spirits might be fighting amongst
themselves"—but not in any sort of negative way that disturbed
the castle's living inhabitants. François felt that perhaps Mr.
Henderson doesn't mind people so much but is less tolerant of
other spirits coming into his home.

François also had a number of secondhand stories to tell me.
An employee told him that a number of years ago, a spiritualist
medium working with the FBI on a cold case visited Henderson
Castle. While at the castle, the medium offered to do a reading
to see if she could get in touch with any spirits who might be
there. The owners agreed and the medium was able to contact
Mr. Henderson. She said that Mr. Henderson told her he was
very upset with a four-year-old child he called "little Christine"
because she had written something on the ceiling. That was as
much information as she was able to get, however.

Perplexed by the tale, François called Fred Royce, the former
owner, to ask if he knew anything about "little Christine" or
writing on the ceiling. Fred told François that, yes, there *had*
been some writing on the ceiling that they found when he was

renovating. "Fred told me that they tried to remove it, sand it, revarnish it, but the writing always came back."

But that wasn't the end of the story. Two months ago, François told me that a paranormal investigation team visited him. One of the women told him that she had visited the castle when she was a little girl and that she had a "secret friend" there who played with her—a four-year-old girl named Christine.

"So there you have two independent stories with Christine," said François. I had to admit, I was becoming convinced myself that there might be something to the story.

"And then," François told me, "in December or January, during a Murder Mystery weekend, one of the guests came to me to show me a photograph she'd taken on the stairs." He pointed to the wide staircase leading up to the second floor. Over the stairs is a huge stained glass window. "I looked at the photo and thought 'that's Mr. Henderson!'" François explained that the apparition was very clear and looked just like the portrait he'd seen of Mr. Henderson in the basement. The guest assured him that when she took the picture, there was no one standing there.

François ended our conversation by reaffirming that whatever spiritual activity he's got in the castle is "very positive," and he feels that Mr. Henderson's spirit has been a beneficial influence on the property.

I asked if it was all right to have a look around. François welcomed me to go into any of the open rooms and walk around the grounds. Before I left he called me back into his office. While I'd been soaking up the Victorian charm of Henderson Castle, François had been busy looking up the website of the paranormal investigators who had visited the castle previously. The Holmes-Yates Paranormal Explorers came out over Labor Day weekend in 2011 and conducted a thorough investigation. You can read the details for yourself on their website: hype paranormal.com.

CHAPTER 16

The National House Inn
MARSHALL

SITTING RIGHT IN THE MIDDLE of Marshall, on the southwest corner of the traffic circle surrounding the beautiful Brooks Memorial Fountain, stands the oldest operating bed-and-breakfast in Michigan. Built in 1835 by Colonel Andrew Mann, The National House Inn is the oldest brick building in the United States and the oldest business in the Marshall/Battle Creek area. It is also believed to have been a stop on the Underground Railroad.

During its first few decades, the inn went through changes of ownership and several names, until it finally had to close its doors in 1878. At that time, it was converted into a factory. Then, in 1902, the building was purchased by a local veterinarian who remodeled the building into eight luxury apartments. "Dean's Flats," as it was known at the time, survived into the latter half of the 20th century, but like so many other old buildings, it eventually fell into disrepair. In 1976, Norm and Kathryn Kinney came to the rescue of the old building and offered to restore the inn to its original purpose. It was a huge and largely volunteer effort, but on Thanksgiving Day of that same year, The National House Inn officially opened for business.

With such a long and varied history, it's little wonder there have been stories circulating on the Internet for years about it being haunted.

When I arrived, innkeeper Barb Bradley greeted me with a warm smile and welcoming "hello." Barb has worked at the inn since 1982 and has been an owner since 1994, so if anyone would know whether or not there was any truth to the rumor of the building being haunted, it would be Barb.

I explained the reason for my visit, and she nodded, telling me that, yes, every once in a while, someone asks about the inn's supposed ghosts. She invited me to sit down with her in the dining room, just off the foyer. The dining room is reminiscent of a cozy country kitchen, so I was surprised later when she said that sometimes they seat as many as 30 guests there. It wasn't that it wasn't a big room, it just felt more like sitting down in a favorite relative's kitchen than a hotel dining room.

"My take on our ghost stories is pretty lighthearted," Barb told me. "But that's just me; I'm a lighthearted person. And the truth is that I've never believed in ghosts or even been interested, or anything like. I know that might seem a little unusual," she added with a smile. "Running an old building like this, it seems like some people just assume I'm also interested in the ghosts that seem to go hand in hand with places like this, but I'm not. What I love is running the inn, entertaining guests, making them feel welcome. For me it's all about the inn, the restoration and preservation of the building, and creating a comfortable, beautiful place for guests to come and enjoy our little town. Of course," she added with a smile, "that doesn't mean I don't *hear* ghost stories from our guests. I'm just not sure I believe in them."

I assured Barb that I wasn't out to prove or disprove anything or to change anybody's minds one way or the other about what they believed. I was just interested in the stories she'd heard over the years.

"Probably the most famous story is the one about the lady in the red dress," she began. She also assured me that it was completely fabricated. "There are some other stories that might be true, but the lady in the red dress is just a local legend. Anyway, the story goes that there was this woman . . . a prostitute who used to work in the area, back when the house was really run down. Nobody is exactly sure when that was; the house was in sad shape for a long time. But, anyway, the story is that this woman died here. People who believe the legend think she still haunts the building. What I think is that maybe because they believe it, their minds are open to it, so if someone sees something out of the corner of their eye or maybe catches a glimpse of something out the window that looks like it might be red, they think it must be the lady in red. But I can tell you that I've been here for more than 20 years, and I've never seen her."

But what Barb *could* tell me about the inn was far more interesting than an old urban legend.

"When I first started here—I think I'd been here for less than a week—my boss, a really wonderful man named Steven Poole, came to me and said that there was a group coming up to the inn from the University of Michigan. They were going to hold a séance here in the parlor, and did I want to join them? She went wide-eyed at the memory, although she was laughing too. "Well, I didn't know what to say except '*no.*' I could hardly believe anyone would ask something like that. Steven told me that I wasn't the only one—he'd asked all the staff, and hardly anyone wanted to be a part of it."

"I'm not sure I blame you," I told her.

"Well, the next day Steven was really nervous even talking about what had happened here the night before. He said it was *so real* and that the things he witnessed didn't have any kind of logical explanation. I really wish I would have been here, just to see what had him so unnerved. The one story he did tell me was that these people who came up from the University of Michigan to study the house told him that there were two people—spirits, I guess—in the house. It's an older couple and they 'live' upstairs in the Dickey Room. They're very peaceful," she said. "But they're very much there. That makes that room the most haunted room in the house. When I have guests who call wanting to rent a room for the night because of the spirits who are supposed to 'live' here, that's always the room they ask for."

Barb also said that the investigators from the university told her former boss that a death had taken place in the house, at the top of the back staircase. The investigators claimed to have felt the spirit of someone who had been murdered there, but weren't able to be any more specific than that. Given the house's long history, it seemed unlikely that they would be able to confirm the report.

"Those are probably the strongest stories—but there is one other that was quite moving. It was the middle of a really busy breakfast, the dining room was full, and this couple who had been staying with us for a few days came downstairs, all bundled up in their coats. It was winter," she explained. "They were ready to check out, but they didn't want to leave until they had a private word with me. I was sure that something must be wrong, maybe something had happened with the plumbing or a light fixture or . . . something. What I wasn't prepared to hear was that they had been in touch with this spirit, this little ghost boy named Jason, all during their stay. They said he was all alone because nobody else could see him, so he had no one to talk to, and that he'd been there since the late 1800s. They said that they would be back when they could, but in the meantime, could I please talk to Jason, so he wouldn't be so lonely. I didn't know quite what to say to that," she confessed.

I'm not sure I would have known what to say to that either.

Barb said she handled it as gracefully as she could by saying something to the effect that since she wasn't the person who had received the message, maybe she wasn't the best person to ask. "That was over 13 years ago, but I still remember it like it was yesterday," she told me. "They were so sincere, and it was *so* real for them. Because it was about a child, I couldn't help but feel moved too, but just didn't know what to do with it."

A couple of paranormal groups have investigated the inn and have come up with evidence of activity—but Barb's favorite "investigators" were a couple of young boys who used to come around the outside of the inn during the 1980s. "It was right after the movie *Ghostbusters* came out. These little guys would dress up in their coveralls and they had little props—and they were very polite," she added. "They never bothered us or the guests or asked to come inside. They would just walk around the outside of the property looking for ghosts." We both laughed.

Before I left, Barb showed me around the rest of the inn, taking me upstairs and letting me have a look at some of the bedrooms. The National House Inn is truly a lovely place with a very sweet innkeeper, and I am definitely planning to go back for an overnight stay sometime soon, so I can explore more of the city.

Marshall was named by the National Trust of Historic Preservation as one of their "Dozen Distinctive Destinations"—not just for Michigan but for the entire country. Marshall is definitely one of the most beautiful cities in Michigan, full of gorgeous 19th-century architecture and a rich cultural history—*and* there's a walking tour of haunted buildings that includes private homes. The office for Marshall Ghost Tours is just a few short blocks down from The National House Inn, and, yes, the inn is on one of the tours offered. You can bet that when I go back to Marshall for another visit, I'll be indulging both my love of things that go bump in the night *and* my love of old buildings—I'm definitely signing up for the tour that includes private homes. The Marshall Ghost Tour is the first one I've found that includes residences.

CHAPTER 17

Regent Theatre
ALLEGAN

WE'VE ALL HEARD THE EXPRESSION "persistence pays off," but never were those words so true for me than the day I returned to the western shore of Michigan. Although I stopped in at a couple of interesting places the day I visited Kalamazoo and Henderson Castle, my other errands prevented me from doing much more than making a few cursory inquiries. One of the places I stopped at was Stuart Manor in Portage, near Kalamazoo. Unfortunately, the woman who knew the most about the manor's resident spirits was out for the day, but I left a message on her voicemail, and a couple of days later we connected via telephone. We set up a time to meet—but when I arrived, I discovered that she'd had something come up last-minute and would have to reschedule. I was a little disappointed, but I had a pretty long list of places to visit over the two days I'd set aside for exploring, so I hit the highway again and traveled to the next stop on my list.

Not only did I strike out at my next stop, but also the stop after that didn't yield any interesting stories either. I was seriously thinking about packing it in and going home to my husband and dog, but as I looked at my map, I thought, "I'm here anyway, so I might as well try *one* more stop. Allegan is only a half an hour up the road. If there's nothing there, I'll grab a hotel for the night and head home in the morning."

When I called my husband to check in later, I exclaimed that I'd hit pay dirt and told him he wouldn't see me until the next afternoon, at the earliest; I had a lot of ground to cover.

Allegan is a quiet little town that straddles the Kalamazoo River, about 30 miles north and west of Kalamazoo. My destination was in the heart of Allegan's historic district—but truth be told, none of the homes and buildings I passed looked younger than a hundred years old. I arrived around 6:30 p.m., perfect timing for my visit to the Regent Theatre, an old cinema house that didn't open its doors until 7 p.m. There was practically no traffic on the streets of Allegan, and about half the shops were already closed up for the day.

I had little difficulty finding a parking spot (although the one-way streets were a little tricky) and took some time to walk around. If nothing else, I was at least getting some really great photographs of beautiful old buildings. One of the most striking was the Regent itself.

Originally built in the late 1800s as a livery stable, the Regent Theatre has gone through numerous renovations and reinventions over the past century, starting in 1902 when the stable was converted into a Buick garage. It wasn't until 1919 that the building was used as a theater, initially for vaudeville.

Then, in the 1930s, the Regent was redecorated in the popular Art Deco style and reopened as a silent-movie house. Much like the Baldwin, which I had toured earlier in the month, the Regent was eventually converted to "talkies"—but fell into disuse in the 1980s. Within a decade, it was slated for demolition and would most likely not be standing were it not for the efforts of the Old Regent Theatre Company, which purchased the property in 1990. The nonprofit organization comprised mainly of volunteers rescued the once-beautiful old building and began the monumental task of renovation. The plan was to restore the theater to the way it had looked in the 1930s. The operation took six years, and in 1996 the Regent, which now shows first-run movies, had its grand reopening.

During these renovations the ghosts who haunt the theater were "woken up" or somehow provoked into making themselves known. Pretty much everyone I've talked to over the course of writing this book has indicated that spirits don't like change. I guess some people are as stubborn in death as they are in life. The Regent has been the subject of several paranormal investigations and has been visited by both the West Michigan Ghost Hunter's Society and the Ghost Research Society. The West Michigan Ghost Hunter's Society posted on their website (located under "historical sites") several orb photographs taken by team members in the lobby of the Regent.

There have been reports of cold spots and a generally "eerie feeling" throughout the building—but most of the evidence I found online was a bit scant, so I was hoping to find someone who could tell me more. I approached the lobby with a sense of nostalgia—the Regent reminded me a lot of the little movie house we used to go to when I was a kid. Stepping into the lobby foyer felt very much like taking a step back in time. I made my way over to the ticket booth and was greeted with a warm smile. Apparently, I was the first customer of the night.

Projection booth window.

I explained that I wasn't really there to see a movie, I was writing a book on haunted places in Michigan, and the Regent had come up in my research.

"We're haunted, all right," said the young woman in the ticket booth. "Hang on a minute, let me get Alicia, she's our manager. She can tell you more than I can."

While I waited patiently for the manager to come down, I had a look around the lobby, where a number of newspaper articles detailing the theater's history were on display. From one of them, I learned that while there were a number of paid employees—all local teenagers—all of the adults on staff were volunteers. I also discovered that despite its antiquated appearance, the Regent shows only first-run movies—admittedly, only one at a time. I also couldn't help but notice that the prices at the concession stand where at least 50 percent less than in any cinema I'd been to in a very long time.

Presently, a young woman in blue jeans and a T-shirt came down the stairs and introduced herself as Alicia. She apologized for keeping me waiting and asked how she could help with my book.

"I'm travelling around Michigan talking to people who work in reputedly haunted places," I told her. "And was wondering if you've ever experienced anything unusual or had anyone tell you about anything unusual."

"I know a guy supposedly had a heart attack in the projection booth. I don't know if it's true or not, but some people have claimed to see a shadowy figure up there," Alicia told me. "I've had people tell me about cold spots or feeling uncomfortable—stuff like that. Sometimes you see things out of the corner of your eye, like a shadow moving, or you just feel like somebody's watching you, or get a weird feeling. In April, the Grand Rapids Paranormal Investigation team is supposed to come out and do a full investigation. It'll be interesting to hear what they find. We're a pretty old building, so it's hard to say if it's haunted or just drafty. Sometimes lights flicker, but that's probably just the wiring."

We talked a little bit about the age of the building and its history for a while, and I learned that a year after its grand reopening, the Regent's roof collapsed. Luckily, no one was hurt, but it was a major setback for the theater. Alicia showed me a picture of the damage—there was a lot of it.

"We had to replace all the seats downstairs, but the ones in the balcony are really cool because they're so old," Alicia told me. I was considering staying for the movie, but then Alicia told me that if I wanted to talk to someone who might know more than she did, I should go across the street; she'd just seen Fred step back into his shop. "His family used to own the theater," she explained.

I thanked Alicia for her time and hurried across the street to the shop she had indicated, the B and C Emporium. The door was locked and the sign flipped to "closed," but I could see the owner near the back, so I knocked. A moment later, Fred opened the door and welcomed me in. I apologized for showing up when he was trying to close and explained Alicia had sent me over in the hopes that I could get some more information about the Regent Theatre's history and its ghosts.

"It's not just the theater—the whole town is haunted," Fred informed me. "There's the ghost dogs that come around after dark. Sometimes they look just like regular dogs, other times you just see part of the dog, just the front half. There used to be a breeder in town," he explained. "And then there's the site of the old Yellow Motel and the Allegan Grill and the Elks Lodge. And I have pictures I've taken myself inside the Griswold Theatre with huge orbs in them," he held his hands apart to demonstrate the size. "I took the pictures myself," he repeated, "so I *know* what's on them, that nobody went in and tampered with it."

Wow. Okay, that's a lot of ghost stories. I asked him if he knew anything about the Regent's ghost.

"Well, we've had several groups out to investigate the Regent Theatre, and I've personally seen the old manager looking out that window there." He pointed to a little window over the theater's neon sign. "That's the projection booth," he said. "The manager died some years ago," he added, "but he's still around." He went on to explain that the manager had been a friend of his family, so, no, he wasn't at all spooked to see him still watching out over the theater. Fred told me that he's heard knocking around in his own shop from time to time, when there's no one around. He's checked for raccoons and other vermin but not seen evidence that they might be responsible for the noises that periodically come from his upstairs.

"You know that Al Capone used to visit Allegan, don't you?" Fred asked me.

No, I hadn't known that, but I was intrigued.

"Oh yeah. They say he stayed at the Yellow Motel." He shrugged. "There's no proof, but lots of rumors, guys showing up in black cars in the middle of the night, that kind of thing. Some people say there are bodies buried on the grounds of the Yellow Motel." He shrugged again and told me that if I wanted to know more, I could look it up pretty easily online after I settled in for the night. He also told me about his friend, fellow Allegan resident Kass Hillard, who conducts "ghost walks" through town around Halloween. She's the cofounder of Michigan Paranormal Encounters and has organized a number of paranormal events in town.

Before we parted company, Fred gave me directions to the Griswold, which is just a few blocks from the Regent. No one was around, but the library was right next door, so I stopped in and talked to one of the librarians for a little while. She was very helpful, and I took a few hours to do some research before heading off to find a hotel for the night.

I discovered some pretty wild stories regarding both the living and the dead, as well as their activities at the Yellow Motel and in the surrounding woods. Several reputable sources, however, did note that Al Capone spent time in western Michigan in the 1920s and may well have visited Allegan, which is only about 150 miles from Chicago. Capone moved to Chicago in the early 1920s and is only one of the city's less-than-reputable citizens to have visited western Michigan.

The Yellow Motel is no longer standing, but all of the other places Fred told me about are still around and open to the public—although some, like the Griswold Theatre, don't keep any sort of regular hours. It was dusk when I left the library, and I took a walk along the waterfront plaza downtown, hoping to catch a glimpse of some ghost dogs, but while plenty of ordinary canines marked my passing by barking at me, there were no ghosts to be seen that night. Just the same, I've decided to come back to Allegan again sometime, as I've completely fallen in love with the town.

CHAPTER 18

Grill House Restaurant
ALLEGAN

BEFORE LEAVING ALLEGAN, I decided to swing by the Grill House Restaurant. If I'd paid closer attention to the menu online before heading out, I probably would have skipped my fast-food lunch. But I had a lot of ground to cover before heading home that night, and I didn't want to stop for a meal, even though the Grill House was only about a ten-minute drive from the motel where I had stopped for the night—a decidedly not-haunted Budget Host.

Later, when I was researching the Grill House's history, I discovered that they have been featured on the Travel Channel's program *Food Paradise*. After I finally had the chance to peruse their menu, I could see why. Beyond the traditional grill-house fare of steaks and chicken, the chefs serve up gourmet pizzas and daily specials, such as Mexican Monday and Italian Tuesday. The main menu features items like beer-battered French fries and a "meal splitter special," where two people get to split an entrée, but each receives a full serving of side dishes.

The next time I'm in the neighborhood, I think I'm going to stop in for "scraps and squid"—steak nuggets and calamari. If I manage to drag my husband with me, we may have to come after 4:30 p.m., when the grill is ready, because the Grill House features something I'd never heard of before: a grill-your-own-steak option. Expert grill masters are on hand to coach customers through the experience—not that my husband would need the help; he's a chef, but he'd probably have a lot of fun. Apparently, grill-your-own-steak restaurants are more popular in Iowa, where Grill House owner Marcia Wagner grew up. Customers can even order butcher-shop quality meat to take home with them.

Originally known as the Hubbard House, the huge, old farmhouse was built in 1836 by Samuel Hubbard, a Massachusetts Supreme Court judge. Hubbard was one of the driving forces behind the settlement of the village of Allegan and built the farmhouse as a boardinghouse for lumberjacks who were coming into the area looking for work in the newly established town. The Hubbard House was the very first public lodging and saloon built in Allegan.

The current owners, Marcia and her husband Dan, purchased the property in 1998 and made several renovations. Firm believers in "shopping locally," the Wagners ran into an unusual problem in 2003 when they were helping their daughter plan her wedding. There wasn't a venue in town large enough to host the event—so they built one! The Silo banquet hall stands where the old barn used to stand, just behind the Grill House, and is described on the hall's website as "a Grand Ballroom that exemplifies elegance in the country."

I pulled into the parking lot just a few minutes before the restaurant opened at 11:00 a.m. The huge, old building looked very much like the farmhouse it used to be, complete with a large front porch—although the entrance was actually off to the side, adjacent to the parking lot. The door was unlocked, so I ventured inside where I found a young man mopping the stairs that led up to the main dining room. I explained the reason for my visit, and he told me to go on up and ask for Brian. I headed toward the bar and was immediately taken by the Grill House's elegant décor. Rather than a rustic farmhouse, the interior of the Grill House reminded me of an upscale restaurant, with antiques (or at least replicas), white table cloths, and pastel painted walls—however, the casual attire and warm greeting of the wait staff made me feel completely "at home." It seemed to me as if the Wagners definitely got it right when they called their restaurant "elegance in the country."

The waitresses smiled when I explained why I was there. They told me that "yes, the place is definitely haunted, and, yes, Brian is who you want to talk to." They offered me a seat and something to drink while I waited for Brian to come down from the office.

I learned that Brian was not only the manager but also the Wagners' nephew, and that he had lived onsite for a while, moving into the living quarters upstairs with his aunt and uncle to help them run the place. He was very gracious about talking to me and moved us over to a table in a closed section of the dining room where it was quieter. Brian asked me if I was familiar with the legend of the Grill House's ghost, "Jack," and I had to confess that I wasn't. I had only just heard about them the day before.

Brian explained, "He was a lumberjack, which is why we call him 'Jack', even though that probably wasn't his real name.

Balcony of the apartment above the restaurant, where the Wagners
found a mysterious scorch mark.

Back then people didn't have much regard for lumberjacks.
They were considered less than human, because they spent so
much time away from town, out in the woods, and lived pretty
rough. So when they came into town, there was almost always
a fight. Jack was knifed downstairs in the bar, and his body was
dumped somewhere in the woods on the property. Or at least
that's the story." It didn't seem as if Brian doubted the tale. "I
was a skeptic before I started working here," he told me. "But
not anymore. Jack's remains have never been found, so that's
probably why he's still here," he added.

I asked Brian what kinds of things people have experienced
in the restaurant.

"All kinds of stuff. Some of it can be explained—like sometimes a glass will fall off a shelf or lights will flicker, but things
like that can happen anywhere, and the building is over a hundred years old. But there was one incident that nobody could
ignore." Brian went on to tell me about how one night, when

things were fairly slow, a customer witnessed four clear glass mugs, the heavy ones used for coffee drinks, fly off the shelf. "The bartender wasn't in the room when it happened, but several customers swore to her that no one was standing anywhere near the shelf when they fell and shattered."

I've worked in restaurants and bars, and glasses don't generally come flying off the shelves—especially not four of them at once—so I was pretty impressed. We talked a little about some of the other places I've visited while working on the book and a little bit about the hospitality business in general. Brian leaned in a little. "Then you'll probably appreciate this one. We had a waitress here that no one really liked—she just wasn't cut out to be a waitress, if you know what I mean."

Oh, most definitely. Waiting tables takes a very special personality and not everybody has it.

"Apparently, Jack didn't like her much either. It seemed as if every single time she passed by the broom it would fall on her. It's one of those old, wood-handled brooms. I mean, it wasn't heavy enough to hurt her, but there was no reason for it to fall on her *all the time*. Once, you could say 'okay' and shrug it off, but six or seven times? Eventually, she quit. That's about the only time Jack's been 'mean' to anyone—and no one was upset to see her go."

By then, I was thoroughly intrigued and asked Brian if he'd ever had any experiences himself, since he used to live there.

"I never really saw anything, even though other people have claimed to see Jack, you know, like a misty apparition. There's one story of people seeing him on the dance floor downstairs, dancing with a woman dressed in Victorian-era clothes—so maybe he found some kind of happiness in the afterlife." Of course, being a romantic at heart, I couldn't help but smile a bit myself.

"But there were a couple of things that happened to me," Brian went on. "I was in the office upstairs—it was winter, and it can be a little drafty, but suddenly I was just freezing cold. The first thing that went through my head was 'how in the heck did the window get open?' Only the window *wasn't* open. Some of the ghosthunters who have been out investigating the place say that that cold feeling you get is a ghost passing through you. I know that sounds a little silly." He shrugged. "All I know is that the window was closed and I was freezing."

"There was another time," Brian began with another story, "when I was locking up at night. The lights sometimes go on and off by themselves—and sometimes the radio stations change all by themselves. Or I guess it's Jack. Usually the bartenders let him have his way and leave the station it changes too—if they don't, he just changes it back. Anyway," he said, resuming his original train of thought, "one night I was closing up, going through and turning off all the lights. The bar has track lighting, with each row of lights on its own switch. You flip one and all the lights on that track turn on or off. I was walking through and one single light turned on, lighting up the corner. I gotta tell you, that one freaked me out just a little."

There were other stories too. Jack has been known to move chairs and, once in a while, when the staff is clearing tables, they'll find a single shot of whiskey on a table that everyone is absolutely certain hadn't been occupied—at least not by any mortal patrons. Whiskey was Jack's drink, so sometimes when a regular customer comes in, they'll order a shot and leave it on the bar for Jack.

It's not just the patrons who appreciate Jack's presence. Brian told me that one day while he was still living on site, he and his aunt and uncle went out for a few hours to run errands. When they got back, they discovered a huge scorch mark on their apartment balcony. It looked like a bunch of leaves had caught fire—but just as mysteriously as it had started, it had stopped. There hadn't been any rain that day. "Somebody was looking out for us," Brian told me. "Maybe it was Jack."

He told me that when they were doing the groundbreaking for the Silo, his aunt and uncle half expected to find Jack's remains. They were relieved when they didn't. I could pretty easily see where that might not be the kind of thing one would want to find on their property, even if they already know it's there.

Before I left, I asked Brian if it would be all right if I took a few photographs of the interior as well as the outside. He welcomed me to take as many pictures as I wanted and wished me a good rest of the day. The Grill House was definitely one of the friendliest places I'd visited—and I really do hope to get back to actually have a meal there.

Spotlight On: The Ada Witch

No book about haunted places in Michigan would be complete without at least some mention of the Ada Witch, who is perhaps one of western Michigan's most famous ghosts. It is unclear how the title "witch" got attached to her name—or even what her true name might be—but that's what locals call the adulterous specter who is believed to haunt Findlay Cemetery and Honeycreek Road, in Ada Township. Ada is a small community, located a little over ten miles east of Grand Rapids, and was first settled in 1821. It was in those early years that many believe the so-called "witch" met her tragic end, an end she may have brought upon herself.

One website dedicated exclusively to the legend of the Ada Witch claimed that she died in the year 1868. It is impossible to verify that date, however, as neither the woman's name nor the actual whereabouts of her grave are known for certain. We can only speculate.

The story says that the woman known as the Ada Witch was having an extramarital affair and would meet secretly with her lover in the marshes outside of town, near what is now Honeycreek Road. When her husband became suspicious of her late-night comings and goings, he followed her and caught her in the arms of her lover. In a jealous rage, the husband murdered first his wife and then the other man. During the struggle with his wife's lover, the husband was also fatally wounded and died a short while later. Perhaps that's why some people report not only seeing a mysterious ghostly woman wandering the area, but also a pair of ghostly men—maybe the men are the Ada Witch's husband and her lover.

The woman is believed to be buried in Findlay Cemetery, but nothing is noted in the stories about where either of the two men might have been interred. Although no one can prove that the gravestone is hers, locals believe that a broken old headstone near the back of Findlay Cemetery is that of the legendary Ada Witch. Visitors often light candles or leave trinkets for her.

Several paranormal investigators have been to the cemetery and believe that it is indeed haunted. There is evidence in the form of orb photos and other unusual phenomena that have been caught on film and on digital cameras. Of course, just as there are many people who believe the story is true, there are just as many who think the Ada Witch is little more than an urban legend.

CHAPTER 19

Kirby House
GRAND HAVEN

I LEFT THE GRILL HOUSE in Allegan and headed north up M-40 through Holland and eventually up to Grand Haven. It was a perfect spring morning, ideal for an hour-long drive up Michigan's western coast. Located on the shore of Lake Michigan, Grand Haven is a popular tourist destination, especially in summer when vacationers seek out the warm sandy beaches and romantic sunsets over Lake Michigan. In September, visitors can indulge in the culinary delights of Grand Haven's annual Salmon Festival, which coincides nicely with the grape harvest and wine tastings offered by local wineries. For those who don't mind the cold, Grand Haven offers a Winterfest complete with dogsled races and an annual photography contest. February sees more winter fun when the city's streets are filled with ice sculptures during the Ice Festival.

But I was in western Michigan on the hunt for ghosts—or at least ghost stories—and Grand Haven seemed to have a lot to offer. Originally, I had just planned to visit the Kirby House Grill, but when I was doing research at the Allegan library the night before, a second restaurant came up, Dee-Lite Bar & Grill. Seeing as the two were located only a few dozen yards from one another on Washington Street, I decided to visit both.

Navigating downtown Grand Haven proved a little bit tricky, mostly because MapQuest's idea of the "easiest route" and mine are not at all the same, but in short order I was pulling up to the curb on Washington Street to park my car. I decided to head down to the Kirby first. Standing on the corner of Washington and Harbor Drive, the attractive two-story, gray-and-yellow building looked more like a modern pub than a place I would likely find ghosts. The interior reminded me of a modern pub, but still feeling hopeful, I went to the hostess stand and waited for someone to come over.

While I waited, I glanced through the menus. The Kirby House is actually three restaurants tucked into a single two-story building on the corner of Washington and Harbor Drive. There's the Kirby Grill, a casual family restaurant; the Grill Room, a traditional-style steakhouse; and the K2, a wood-fired-oven pizzeria that serves up a variety of interesting specialty pizzas, including a Thai pizza with peanut sauce, chicken, carrots, and cucumbers, and a lobster carbonara pizza. As carbonara happens to be my favorite, I figured that even if there weren't any ghost stories to be found, lunch was definitely in order before I left Grand Haven!

But first to work. When the hostess, a young woman named Lillian, came my way, I gave her a friendly smile and explained why I was visiting.

"You should really talk to Tim," she advised me. "He'll be in later tonight if you want to come back."

I winced. I really had to get back on the road as soon as I wrapped up in Grand Haven, and while I had every intention of having lunch before I left, sticking around town until evening was out of the question.

"Have *you* ever seen anything?" I asked Lillian, hopefully. "Or maybe some of your customers or coworkers have told you about things they've seen or heard that might seem a little unusual?" I have found that sometimes when people are reluctant to open up at first, keeping the conversation going for a few more minutes helps to get them talking.

Lillian hesitated another second before deciding that it would probably be okay for her to take me downstairs to see where Emily's room used to be. Emily is the Kirby's resident spirit. She may have been a guest of the original Kirby Hotel—but that's just a guess; no one actually knows for sure who she was, just that she died in the building.

"Emily was coming down those steps, there." Lillian pointed to the wide staircase behind the hostess stand. "And she tripped on the hem of her gown and tumbled to her death."

Built in 1873 by renowned hotelman Edward Killean, the Kirby House was a hotel for many years before changing hands—and names. The building has had many owners and names over the last century, before finally being purchased by Gregory Gilmore in 1989. Gilmore returned the establishment to its original name, if not its original purpose, and it has been enjoying financial and culinary success ever since, despite—or perhaps because of—the ghost stories.

A few people claim to have seen Emily's ghost on the stairs, but more frequently, patrons and employees report hearing a small child's footsteps walking up and down the stairs or running around in the pizzeria upstairs. A few people have even reported seeing a little boy running around up there—others have said they simply saw a "shadow move," but when they turned around, no one was there.

Despite all the reports of ghostly experiences on the second floor, it was the basement Lillian wanted to show me. She got someone to cover her station for a few minutes and led the way, chatting as we went. "Customers over at the bar say all the time that they feel someone tugging at their legs or arms. Sometimes we tell her 'Emily, stop it!'" Lillian told me, with as much conviction as if she were talking about a coworker—or maybe an errant child.

"Does that work?" I asked.

"Usually."

The storage area Lillian took me to is off-limits to the general public, but the basement itself is open to patrons. Following Lillian down the darkened wooden steps, I was hard-pressed not to feel a little bit of apprehension—but maybe that was just because I knew we were headed to Emily's room.

"A lot of people hear loud banging down here," Lillian said, as we stepped inside and she hit the light. The storage area looked pretty much like any restaurant's storeroom I'd ever been in before. "But whenever anyone goes to check it out, there's no one down here. There aren't any animals or anything either."

The place certainly looked clean enough; I wouldn't have suspected vermin. Besides, doesn't it take something bigger than a few mice to make "loud banging" noises?

"Some people won't come down here alone," Lillian told me. "I always feel like she's watching me, especially down in here." She led the way to the very back of the storeroom. By then we both had goose bumps. Lillian shivered. "Sometimes she turns the lights off and on, and doors sometimes open and shut by themselves. We've had a few things fall off shelves in the kitchen, but it's hard to tell if that's really Emily or just normal stuff that happens in a restaurant."

Later, while I was researching the Kirby House's history to write this chapter, I discovered an interesting connection between the restaurant and another one of Grand Haven's famous ghosts, the "Blue Man of Lake Forest Cemetery." Apparently, before Edward Killean built the Kirby House hotel, the land was owned by the Ferry family. Reverend William Ferry was one of Grand Haven's founding fathers. He built the very first permanent dwelling in town and lived there with his wife, Amanda, where the Kirby now stands. The Ferry's home burned to the ground in 1866, and the couple moved. A few years later, Reverend Ferry passed away and was buried on Founders' Hill, in the Lake Forest Cemetery. Local legend has it that his spirit appears to cemetery visitors as a glowing blue apparition. The story may just be an urban myth, but the Lake Forest Cemetery is on my list of places to visit the next time I'm in the area, as it is within easy driving distance of Grand Haven.

CHAPTER 20

Dee-Lite Bar & Grill
GRAND HAVEN

I LEFT THE KIRBY HOUSE RESTAURANT and walked a few hundred feet down Washington Street toward the Dee-Lite Bar & Grill. Between the two restaurants stood the Grand Theatre—or at least what was left of it. The Grand Theatre first opened for business on January 23, 1928, and seated 800 people. Both motion pictures and stage productions played there, and by all accounts the Grand was a major theater with patrons coming from all over western Michigan. But as all good things do, its heyday ended and the theater fell into decline, finally closing its doors for good in 1999, when the property fell into foreclosure. While the façade and marquee still remain, the theater itself was torn down in 2005, and loft-style condominiums were built in its place. Where the theater's lobby used to stand, visitors will now find the Grand Theatre Seafood and Oyster Bar.

Next to that stood my destination, the Dee-Lite Bar & Grill. Although the place has been in operation since 1937, the first thing I thought when I saw it was "1950s diner." From the style of the bright neon letters to the clock over the sign outside and the interior with its big comfortable booths and chrome bar stools, the restaurant is a tribute to a bygone decade. The menu, however, proved to be anything but antiquated. Featured items included both standard American diner fare, including breakfast served all day, as well as Tex-Mex entrées and Monday night sushi. I definitely know where I'm going for dinner if I make it back up to Grand Haven on a Monday! For entertainment, Sundays at Dee-Lite bring the blues, Monday open mic night, and on Tuesday, patrons can enjoy live jazz music in the adjacent Grand Theatre Seafood and Oyster Bar.

It was about two o'clock in the afternoon when I walked into Dee-Lite, and right away I noticed a couple of waitresses sitting in one of the back booths, rolling silverware. That was a sight that brought back memories—I waited tables all through college and for some years later, mostly in places like the Dee-Lite Bar & Grill, although none of them were reputed to be haunted.

I walked over and introduced myself with a smile, explaining the reason for my visit. "I'm writing a book about haunted places in Michigan, and the restaurant came up in my research. I was wondering if you knew anything about it."

"His name is John," said one of the ladies, her tone completely matter of fact. The nametag on her uniform read "Jessica"—the other gal's name was Shawna. Neither waitress was the least bit shy when it came to talking about their ghost. "He used to be the custodian at the old Grand Theatre," Jessica told me.

"He died," Shawna added.

John Buchanan was the first custodian to have been employed by the Grand Theatre back in the late 1920s, and he worked there for almost 40 years. He passed away in 1975, after which theater employees started claiming that the place was haunted. Before the Grand was torn down, employees reported hearing odd noises throughout the theater and swore lights turned on and off by themselves. Employees even reported that trash would be mysteriously cleaned up when no one was supposed to be working. I wondered briefly if I could get John Buchanan to come home and clean my house.

Could it be that even though the theater was long gone, John Buchanan remained on the property and was haunting the Dee-Lite?

The waitresses at Dee-Lite sure seemed to think so. I was intrigued and asked them what sorts of experiences they'd had.

"I heard John once," Jessica told me. "It was this really creepy sound, and I was totally freaked out by it. I'm not the only person who's heard him either," she insisted.

"What happened?" I asked.

"It was early morning—the restaurant opens at 5 a.m., so we get here pretty early to open. It's always dark out when we get in, and the only light we have in the restaurant when we come in is coming from the street." She nodded to the large glass windows at the front of the restaurant. "We have to turn all the lights on manually; there's no master switch or anything. And it's usually just two of us," she added, "one waitress and a cook. So I was here opening, turning on the lights in the restaurant. I had to go into the bathroom to turn that light on too. And I *swear* I heard the weirdest sound coming from the shadows—"

"And there are lots of shadows around here," Shawna added.

Jessica nodded. "I ran right out of the bathroom and got my cook and made her come with me to finish turning on the lights. I was not going back in there by myself!"

Shawna nodded. "I remember you telling me about it when I came in that day. You said it was this weird inhuman growling sound."

"Yeah," said Jessica. "It *wasn't* natural. It wasn't a person or an animal or . . . or anything *natural*," she insisted.

Okay, so maybe I *didn't* want to hire John to do my housework after all.

Shawna took over the ghost stories for a while. "I've felt really uneasy in here too," she said. "Especially early in the morning when I'm just coming in and the lights are off. It's really creepy . . . . It's like . . . you'll just be getting your work done and then all of a sudden, something will dart out of nowhere, out of the corner of your eye. But then you turn to see what it was, and there's nothing there. That happens all the time."

"We feel stuff too sometimes," Jessica added.

Shawna nodded. "Like I said, in the morning when it's just you and your cook, and you *know* where your cook is, they're banging and clanging in the kitchen making all kinds of noise."

I laughed and agreed. "I'm married to a chef."

Both ladies nodded. "So you know. They're not quiet when they're in the kitchen," said Shawna. "So, one morning I was out here and my cook was in the kitchen banging around, and suddenly I felt like a gust of air, like somebody had just walked past me. It freaked me out pretty good."

Jessica agreed. "You get stuff like that around here all the time. The girls over in the oyster bar see stuff and hear weird stuff a lot too. And sometimes we feel these cold spots, both over here and in the bar. It's like you'll be working and suddenly the temperature just drops for no reason at all."

"There's so much stuff that happens around here," Shawna told me.

She and Jessica went on to relate the story of something that had happened to one of their cooks. Since I don't have her express permission to use her name—she wasn't there for me to ask—I'll just use her initial, V.

V was in the cooler one morning, checking temperatures—just routine maintenance, so she didn't bother turning on all the lights. Apparently, John thought she needed some more light to do her job properly, because suddenly all the lights in the back came on. There wasn't anyone around who could have flipped the switch; V was alone in the back room.

Despite the level of activity and the genuinely scary-sounding noises Jessica heard in the bathroom that one morning, neither she nor Shawna expressed any fear about working in the restaurant. John had never hurt anyone, they assured me; he just unnerved the staff sometimes. All things considered, he sounded a little easier to work with than Emily at the Kirby House Grill.

I thanked Shawna and Jessica for their time and let them get back to their side work. I had to take some pictures of both restaurants, get some lunch, and then hit the road.

CHAPTER 21

Stuart Manor
PORTAGE

I **WRAPPED UP TAKING PHOTOGRAPHS** of the Kirby Grill and Dee-Lite Bar & Grill fairly quickly and was about to call my husband to let him know I would be home early when I noticed a voicemail message for me on my phone. It was from Alison Alexander, the cultural events coordinator for the city of Portage. Alison and I were supposed to have gotten together the day before at Celery Flats, where she'd kindly offered to show me around Stuart Manor. Unfortunately, she had to cancel due to something coming up unexpectedly. She was calling back to see if I wanted to reschedule for that evening. So much for getting home early—then again, it isn't every day I get offered a private tour of a 150-year-old haunted house! So instead of telling my husband I'd be home early, I asked him to do the things on my list of household chores for the night and said I'd see him sometime after dinner because I was meeting Alison around six o'clock. Portage is about 20 minutes south and slightly east of Kalamazoo, which makes it about two-and-a-half hours west of metro-Detroit.

Although Stuart Manor bears the name of former United States Senator Charles E. Stuart, it was actually built by William Welch in 1846, making it the oldest building I had toured so far. It also happens to be the oldest building still standing in Portage. The stately, white Greek Revival house was originally located on Stuart Avenue in downtown Portage, but in 1994 the city moved it to its current location in the Celery Flats Bicentennial Park. It has been fully renovated and oufitted with antique furnishings—except for the modern kitchen. The parks and recreation staff, who oversaw the restoration, needed a modern kitchen in the manor because of the plans to use the building for special events, such as Victorian-style afternoon teas, served on the weekends. In addition to city-sponsored events, Stuart Manor and several other historic buildings in Celery Flats are available for private rental. If I'd known that a few years ago, I probably would have booked my bridal shower there. Not only would it have been Victorian themed, but how much fun would it have been to tell people later about our party in a haunted house?

Celery Flats is described on Portage's website as "a park within a park." On one side of the road, visitors will find the Celery Flats Interpretive Center and Museum, which highlights the importance of celery farming to Kalamazoo County's history. On the other side of the road, park-goers can stroll along a paved walking path that curves past Stuart Manor, an old one-room school house (built in 1856), and a grain elevator, dating from 1931. In addition, many community and cultural events are scheduled at the Hayloft Theatre, a turn-of-the-century barn

that was renovated into a theater in the late 1940s. Like Stuart
Manor, it was also relocated to Celery Flats some years ago.

For visitors who just want to get a little closer to nature,
there are numerous walking paths through the woods on the
other side of the road (which is also a part of the park) and play
areas for small children. Quite a few of Portage's residents were
enjoying evening strolls along Portage Creek as I pulled into the
Celery Flats parking lot for my meeting with Alison. With my
camera in hand, I walked across the street where she met me at
the door of Stuart Manor.

"I'm glad you were able to make it." She greeted me with a
warm smile and welcomed me into the foyer. "We just had the
house painted, so things still aren't quite all back to where they
belong," she added apologetically.

"The house is beautiful," I told her. That wasn't just me being
polite either. Stuart Manor might not be the biggest house I've
ever been in—in fact, by modern standards, it's little more than
average—but I could easily see it as the sort of place a senator
had once called home.

Alison smiled and told me that she had been the person in
charge of selecting the new paint scheme. "The walls were stark
white before this. It was really boring. Not *all* of the new colors
are strictly Victorian, but most of them are."

I was impressed and asked about what kind of research she
had to do to come up with an authentic Victorian color scheme.

Alison laughed. "The paint store had a selection of historical
colors; that made it a lot easier."

Of course, I wasn't actually there to talk about the décor, as
lovely as it was. I was interested in the manor's history and its
ghosts.

Alison showed me the portrait of Charles Stuart, which sits
in the foyer. "We're not 100 percent positive it's him who haunts
the place, but we refer to him as Charles anyway. Of course, we

have a lot of antiques in here from other locations—nothing is original to the Stuart house. Sometimes when we bring new stuff in, we get a rash of paranormal activity." That, of course, was exactly what I'd heard from Pat and Lynn, in Holly, and several other people as well.

"Charles doesn't like his picture being taken down," Alison told me. "It was one of the first things we put back after they painted. Weird stuff always seems to happen whenever we take it down. His portrait used to hang in the main room," she added. "But when we started having teas, we moved him to the foyer." We both agreed that it was a more dignified place for the former owner of Stuart Manor.

Alison showed me into the main room, which probably used to be a front parlor but was currently set up for afternoon tea. Several dining tables were set up around the large room, which also had a lovely upright piano along one wall.

"Do you want to sit down and talk first or see the rest of the house?"

"Would you mind showing me around?"

Before leaving the front room, Alison showed me the modernized kitchen and a little side room set up with one large dining table—which had a lot of china piled on top of it, waiting to be put back. "Sorry about the mess," she said again. The room used to be the family dining room but is now used mostly to store china and silver for afternoon tea.

As we headed toward the stairway, Alison warned me to watch my step. "They built steps pretty steep and narrow back then."

She wasn't kidding. I'm pretty short so I have small feet, and I still nearly tripped going up the narrow steps.

Alison filled me in on a little bit of trivia. "The house is built so that from the outside it only looks like a one-story house—that's why all the windows in the bedrooms sit so low on the wall."

The windows in the bedrooms were practically at knee level.

Portrait of Senator Charles E. Stuart in the foyer of Stuart Manor.

"Back then, you paid higher taxes for a two-story house," said Alison.

She led me into one of the bedrooms.

"We call this room the 'rope room.'" She showed me why. The mattress is held up by a net of ropes. "This is what they used before box springs," she told me. "This is the room that probably gets the most activity. We had groups of Civil War reenactors who rented out the grounds. One of the guys was changing up here, and he came bolting down the stairs. He said he would change anywhere but up here. He never told us why— just that he wasn't comfortable here. But another guy, on a different occasion, said that while he was up here changing clothes someone—or something—touched him. He was up here alone at the time. The story's gotten pretty exaggerated over time, and now people say he was pushed, but that wasn't the story he told at the time."

And that was what made the next part of Alison's recounting of events even more interesting.

"We've had a lot of paranormal investigators come through here," she said. "One of them had heard the story of the guy getting pushed, so when they came into this room, they asked the spirits 'why did you push the soldier?' And the voice on the EVP (electronic voice phenomena) sounded so clear. 'I didn't,' it said."

Okay, I was definitely starting to think there might be something to the ghost at Stuart Manor.

"Sometimes the guys who are doing Civil War reenactments stay overnight. A few of them have sworn they heard someone walking around in the house, even though everyone else was asleep. We've had a bunch of reports from park rangers who come by at night on patrol and find lights turned on when there's no one staying here. They come in, turn the lights off, lock up—and when they swing back by later, the lights are on again. We finally just told them to go ahead and leave the lights on. It's easier on everybody."

Alison showed me the rest of the upstairs, and then we went back down to the main room to have a seat.

"That's Charles's chair," she told me, indicating a particular chair at the largest of the dining tables.

I decided not to sit there, just in case there really was something to the ghost story, and chose a seat on the other side of the table instead. Alison sat down next to me.

"How do you know it's his?" I wondered, remembering that none of the furniture was original to the house.

"We always find that chair pulled out," she explained. And then she smiled and said, "A lot of the people who have done work on the house have heard odd noises, but one time we had an electrician in, working on the light fixture in the original dining room." She nodded to the little room that houses the china cabinets. "He said he came out to get something from his tool box and found Charles's chair pulled out. He didn't think much of it except that it was in his way, so he pushed it back into place and went back to work. He had his back turned to this room, so he didn't see what happened, but when he came back out to get something else, *all* the chairs were pulled out. Now he won't work over here unless I come over and keep him company."

I wasn't sure I blamed the guy. The rooms are directly adjacent to one another; if someone had been trying to put one over on the electrician, they would have to have been awfully quiet for him not to hear them. "Is anyone else uncomfortable being here by themselves?" I asked.

"I never have been," said Alison. "I figure it's just part of working in an old building. Sometimes we find the piano bench pulled out too," she said, indicating the piano I'd been admiring before. "I mean, it's possible that one of the guys working over here likes to play on his breaks or something, but. . . ." She shrugged, leaving me to draw my own conclusions.

And while we were on the subject of chairs, Alison told me that during a private party held at the manor, one of the dining chairs had fallen over. No one was near it at the time; it just fell right on its side for no reason at all—or at least no earthly reason.

"Some of the paranormal investigators have said they found evidence that the schoolhouse is haunted, but I've never experienced anything there." She shrugged. Then she finished off our chat with the story of a mysterious figure people have seen near Stuart Manor, near city hall. "Over by the train tracks people see a woman coming out of the woods and getting into a coach— but then she vanishes. It only happens in the autumn."

I thanked Alison for her time, especially since she'd agreed to meet with me so late in the day and had given me such a great tour of the manor. As I was heading out, I drove past the railroad tracks where so many people say they've seen the ghostly woman boarding her coach. I didn't see anything, but Portage isn't that far from home, so I think I'll try again in the fall. Maybe next time I'll get lucky.

Spotlight On: Nunica Cemetery

When I was visiting with Shawna and Jessica at the Dee-Lite Bar & Grill in Grand Haven, they told me a story about the Nunica Cemetery. A friend of theirs (someone they both described as respectable, honest, and professional, the sort of person not prone to making things up) had relayed to them something unusual. He said that he and a friend were visiting the Nunica Cemetery. For reasons the gals at Dee-Lite weren't clear on, one of the men had his father's cell phone in his pocket rather than his own. Perhaps his was broken, or maybe he'd just picked up his dad's by mistake.

As the two men were walking through the cemetery, they heard what they described as "old-time Gospel music"—the source was the dad's cell phone. But the thing was, Dad was an old-fashioned kind of man with a no-frills phone. He didn't even know how to download music to his phone, so there was no reason for it to be there—and no reason for the phone to have started playing anything anyway.

Neither of the ladies had any explanation for the strange occurrence, but suggested I might want to check out the Nunica Cemetery. What I found was pretty interesting, because apparently the Nunica Cemetery *does* have a reputation as being haunted—in fact, some people claim that it's western Michigan's most haunted cemetery. It's certainly one of the oldest I've ever visited.

There have been numerous reports of voices being heard and cold spots felt all over the cemetery grounds, as well as stories of a "lady in white," a ghostly apparition who is said to appear to visitors from time to time. Orbs and other ghostly phenomena have been photographed in the cemetery. While concrete documentation of the "lady in white" was scarce, I found a number of stories by people who claim to have felt or seen ghostly children running around the cemetery grounds. Upon further investigation, I discovered that in the middle section of the cemetery there were a lot of graves belonging to young children who likely died during an influenza outbreak in the 1920s.

Located in rural western Michigan, ten miles east of Grand Haven, the community of Nunica was founded in 1872. The Nunica Cemetery was established 11 years later, in 1883 and is one of two area graveyards. Like most cemeteries, there are posted "hours of operation," and the police will prosecute trespassers, because having a reputation as a haunted hotspot brings a lot of unwanted attention to the cemetery. Local officials don't object to respectful, responsible adults visiting during the daytime; it's just nighttime visits that are unwelcome. However, as at least one ghosthunter pointed out, if a place is haunted at night, it's just as haunted during the day. There's no reason not to stop in during the posted "open" times, because if nothing else, the Nunica Cemetery is a beautiful old graveyard.

History buffs may want to look for Civil War veteran Henry E. Plant's gravestone while they're there. Plant, a soldier in the Union Army, received the Congressional Medal of Honor for rescuing his unit's colors from Confederate soldiers during a skirmish in 1865.

CHAPTER 22

Sam's Joint
PLAINWELL

I ENDED UP VISITING PLAINWELL and Sam's Joint twice. The first time I was out that way, I stopped in for lunch, but no one seemed to know much about the alleged haunting—in fact, one waitress said she didn't believe that they were haunted.

"It's an old building and stuff happens," she told me.

I could accept that, but I had this feeling that there might be more to the story—not that I thought anybody was lying or trying to hide anything. Maybe I wasn't talking to the right people. I'd encountered a few places before where some staff members believed in ghosts and others didn't. My instincts told me that if I came back, I might have better luck. And as luck would have it, I had business in Kalamazoo again a couple of weeks later. I decided to schedule an extra day on the road to return to Plain-well and have dinner at Sam's Joint.

I arrived fairly early in the evening, but already guests were lined up at the door. When I got to the hostess stand, I told her about the book I was working on and asked if there was some-body I could talk to about the restaurant's ghost stories. She promised to get her manager out to talk to me as soon as she could, but clearly they were swamped. I was more than happy to let other customers go ahead of me.

A couple of guests overheard our conversation, and the gen-tleman told me that the place was absolutely haunted. He said that the area by the restrooms was where I should be looking if I wanted to find ghosts at Sam's Joint. "My wife always feels a little uncomfortable back there—but the food is good, so we keep coming back."

A few minutes later, General Manager Kim Kusmierz came out to talk to me, but several more customers came in the door, so she ended up spending the next few minutes helping the hostess get the line down. In between seating other guests, Kim talked to me, but when it looked like it wasn't going to be pos-sible to carry on any kind of in-depth conversation, she asked if I could come back the next day. "Michelle is on tomorrow night, and she knows more about our ghosts than anybody else here. You could sit right up at the bar and talk to her."

Except for one small problem. "I live in metro-Detroit."

"Oh. Well. . ." she hesitated.

"I was planning to stay for dinner tonight anyway," I explained, "So if maybe you want to find me a spot somewhere, we can talk when things settle down?"

Kim was happy to squeeze me in. "I'll put you in Karen's section. She's kind of busy right now, but she knows quite a bit about it. I'm sure she'll be happy to talk to you as soon as she catches up with her other customers."

That worked for me, and I had a seat in Karen's section, happy to wait for a few minutes for her to get her other tables caught up. In the meantime, Kim finally had a few seconds to come over and sit down with me too.

"I have just enough time to tell you one short story," Kim began. "We had an employee here named Donnie, and . . . well, he had some problems and he shot himself. He left after work one day and he went home, and we never saw him again. It was pretty awful. A bunch of us went to his funeral."

"I'm so sorry," I said.

"Yeah," Kim nodded. "Well, a little while after that, we had some people in who see stuff—you know, spirits. They were sitting at the bar and they said they could see someone over in the doorway, near the kitchen. I asked them what exactly they saw, and they explained that it was a guy standing with one arm crossed over his body, holding onto the opposite elbow. That's the way that Donnie always stood. He never crossed both arms in front of him; it was always just the one. And he used to like to come out and see what was going on in the restaurant too. He'd stand right over there," she added. "He really put his heart and soul into this place when he was alive, so I guess maybe he didn't want to leave us after he died. I've had several people say they saw him too, so I'm convinced he's definitely here."

Kim told me that, at least according to local rumor, there have been a couple tragedies even more directly associated with the building. One story tells of a man who hanged himself in one of the upper rooms. She was never sure whether or not to believe the story, but recently the staff heard a story from one of their customers that just might corroborate it. "A customer came in and mentioned to us that his best friend's brother hanged himself here on the property," said Kim. She told me she's got several staff members that keep a lookout for that particular

A life-size statue of the Blues Brothers greets guests at the hostess stand of Sam's Joint.

customer; the next time he comes in, they're hoping to get some more details from him.

She also told me that when they were remodeling and tore down one of the walls, workers found an old charcoal drawing of a young woman—it's hanging on the wall near the banquet room. "Rumor has it that that she was brutally raped and murdered here, back when this was a stagecoach stop," said Kim.

The building was originally built in 1838 by a man named Calvin White. It was originally called the Red Brick House, but within a few years became known as the Red Brick Tavern. It is one of the oldest structures still standing in Allegan County.

In more recent history, the building must have become a private residence, because Kim told me that one of the former residents is a regular guest of the restaurant. "She comes in every few months," she said. "And one time she told me about how when she was a little girl, maybe eight or ten years old, she and her friends used to hold séances upstairs. They would all sit around this really heavy table—it's still here. The thing must weight a hundred pounds. Anyway, she told me that during their séances, the table would literally lift up off the ground. There's no way a bunch of eight- or ten-year-olds could lift that thing."

Several paranormal investigators have been to Sam's Joint over the years. The most recent group to visit them was the Michigan Night Stalkers, who captured several EVPs (electronic voice phenomena) in the basement. The Night Stalkers told staff members that the young woman whose spirit inhabits the basement was looking for her hairpin, and suggested that someone leave a bobby pin downstairs for her. A report of the Night Stalkers investigation of Sam's Joint, including EVPs and video clips, can be found on their website.

Karen was ready to take my order and to talk to me for a few minutes. She said that she didn't actually believe any of the ghost stories that people told about the restaurant, even though she'd been there since she was 16 working in the kitchen.

"But that doesn't mean that every morning that I open up, I don't stop and say 'Good morning' to whatever might be listening," she told me with a laugh.

While I was waiting for my salad, another waitress stopped by my table to tell me about some of the stories she'd heard, mostly from her customers, which were fairly similar to the things Kim had already told me. She also confirmed that a lot of her customers have reported an "eerie feeling" around the restrooms.

I had to confess that I'd felt a strange feeling when I headed down the long corridor toward the restrooms on my very first visit to Sam's Joint, but the place is so full of old photographs and other unusual items that I had chalked it up to my imagination. The man who owns the restaurant—and seven others like it—is apparently quite a collector of "old curiosities." The walls of the restaurant are literally full of old paintings and portraits, antique instruments, and other odds and ends. There's even a large stained glass window hanging up as wall décor. My favorite piece is the nearly life-sized replica of Blues Brothers, Jake and Elwood, next to the hostess stand.

Just before I left, Kim invited me to phone the next evening to talk to Michelle.

The next night, I phoned Michelle, who has been at Sam's Joint for 16 years and describes the place as very much a family restaurant. Many of the employees are related to one another, or they're all friends, and most of them have been there for a long time.

She began our conversation by asking me exactly what I was looking for.

"Pretty much anything you want to tell me," I said. "Anything that has happened to you over the years that you might consider unusual or anything that a coworker or customer has told you."

"All right. I guess I can start with something that happened about eight years ago. I was closing up the restaurant with one server. I was behind the bar counting out the drawer, and she was sweeping up. We had all the lights off, except for the bar light and the hallway—and there was no one else here," she emphasized. "We didn't hear anything, but all of the sudden we looked at each other because we'd both seen a shadow moving in the hallway." The hallway Michelle was describing runs from the hostess stand toward the kitchen, and along the dining room. "Well, we decided it was time to leave," she told me, "so we finished up as quickly as we could and headed out the door. But before we could actually leave, we had to set the alarm. Now, the alarm system here is all based on motion sensors. Each room has its own motion detector, and the alarm won't set if there's any kind of movement in that room. If there is, there's a code on the keypad to let us know which room has someone walking around or whatever. I start setting the alarm—but it won't arm. The code came up to tell me what room the problem was in, and it was in the area we call the lodge. Now, back then, we had a bunch of model airplanes hanging from the ceiling in the lodge area," she explained. "And I looked up, because from where we were standing, I had a clear view. And there was this *one* model airplane swinging back and forth. Not just moving a little bit—it was swinging," she insisted. "So me and the other gal looked at each other, not knowing how we were going to get the alarm to set with the model plane moving, because neither of us wanted to go down there. But then all of the sudden, the alarm set itself. We looked back up, and the airplane was still. And we locked up and left."

I think I would have too.

"We've had a bunch of little stuff too," Michelle went on. "Have you been in the women's restroom?"

"Oh yeah," I told her, remembering the odd feeling I got the very first time I visited.

"Yeah. I don't go in there by myself. I know that might sound a little dramatic, but I just . . . I won't do it. There's just something about that room that feels cold and eerie to me, so I always make sure I'm not alone."

Michelle told me that she never used to believe in ghosts or spirits, but after working at Sam's Joint for a while, she definitely believes in something.

We talked for a while more, and she elaborated on a few of the stories Kim had told me, including a slightly different version of the story of the man who hanged himself upstairs. Michelle had heard that it had happened when the building was a boarding house, and it was one of the boarders who had taken his own life after he was told he had to move. Apparently, the business had changed hands, and the man was so upset that he took his own life. Regardless of when he died, people have always claimed to see him hanging in one of the upstairs windows.

Whether the different versions of the story mean that there were two suicides inside the building, or if perhaps the stories have just been told in different ways over the years, I couldn't say, but it sounded as if the place has seen a lot of tragedy in one form or another. Michelle did say that things have quieted down a lot the last few years. If the stories of recent occurrences that she, Kim, and other staff members told me were their idea of "quiet," I wasn't sure I would have wanted to be around when they first opened up!

Michelle and I talked a little more, but eventually the bar got busy again and she had to get back to work, but she invited me to come back sometime when she was working. I'm definitely going to take her up on that.

Upper Peninsula

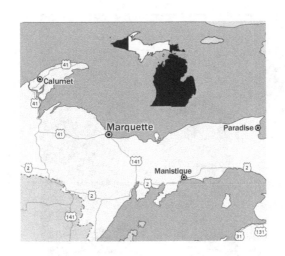

Calumet
  Calumet Theatre

Gulliver
  Seul Choix Point Lighthouse

Marquette
  Landmark Inn

Paradise
  Whitefish Point Lighthouse and Shipwreck Museum

CHAPTER 23

Seul Choix Point Lighthouse
GULLIVER

ALTHOUGH I'VE LIVED ALL MY LIFE in a state where more than 100 lighthouses dot the coastline, I had never actually visited one before venturing to Seul Choix Point, my first stop in the Upper Peninsula. I wasn't sure what to expect when I got there. The Point's hundred-year-old lighthouse is reportedly one of the most haunted places in Michigan and was even featured on an episode of Fox Family's *Scariest Places on Earth*. Even coming straight from spending a relatively quiet night alone at the haunted Blue Pelican Inn (see Chapter 28), I was feeling some trepidation as I approached my next destination. The battered blue sign telling me that Seul Choix's historic lighthouse lay only 2 miles ahead did little to allay the feeling—neither did the slow drive up an old dirt road.

Seul Choix Point is a narrow, rocky stretch of land that juts out from Lake Michigan's northern shore into Seul Choix Bay, about a two-hour drive east of St. Ignace. The bay received its name, which means "only choice," in the 1800s when a group of French fur traders took shelter there during a violent storm that threatened to capsize their small vessel. The bay was their "only choice" for safe refuge along the dangerous stretch of coast, which is known for its rocky shoreline and high waves.

Those same waves make Seul Choix Bay a popular destination for surfers. I found a group of young men out enjoying the waves and warm early autumn weather the day I visited the Point, and took a few minutes to talk to them. They didn't know anything about any ghosts at the lighthouse; they were just out to get in a few more days of lake surfing before the weather turned cold.

The Michigan State Congress commissioned the Seul Choix Point Lighthouse in 1886, but it took six years for it to become operational—I think sometimes we forget how much work went into building construction a century ago. The entire complex, which consists of the 79-foot light tower, family quarters, a steam fog signal and boiler house, stable, and a number of other buildings, wasn't completed until 1895. Additional living quarters were added in 1925. Back then, the Seul Choix Lighthouse was the only guiding light for ships along a hundred-mile stretch of treacherous coastline. The nearest towns are Gulliver—whose Historical Society, in cooperation with the Department of

Natural Resources (DNR), oversees the upkeep of the light-house—and Manistique, a popular destination for boaters, campers, and hikers.

I arrived at the end of the long dirt road to find a well-kept yard, brown brick house, and classic white light tower. Maybe it was the sunny weather, but I didn't feel as if I'd just pulled up in front of one of the "scariest places on earth." Wondering what I was really going to find, I headed over to the gift shop. Rather than asking about ghosts, my first question was, "How do you pronounce the name of this place?"

The young lady behind the counter laughed. It's a question she gets a lot. "The easiest way I know to pronounce it is Sis-shaw," she told me. After getting that cleared up, I explained that I was writing a book about haunted places in Michigan and wondered if she'd ever seen or heard anything unusual in the lighthouse. "Not personally," she said. Although several guests and other staff members told her they'd heard music, "like an old phonograph recording," playing in the lighthouse. She said that some people also report that electronic devices, like the digital camera I was carrying, stop working. "The batteries just die for no reason," she said.

I definitely hoped that wouldn't become a problem. Of course, I always carry extra batteries, just in case.

"If you really want some good stories, it's my mom you should talk to," she went on. "You can find her over at the light-keeper's quarters."

I thanked her for her time and headed on over. The first thing that struck me when I walked into the house was how small the front parlor was. Yet at times in the lighthouse's history, not only did the lightkeeper and his family live there, but his assis-tant and his family resided in the small dwelling as well. That's four adults and as many as six children. The lightkeeper's home has been fully restored and is decorated with beautiful antique

Kitchen at the Seul Choix Point Lighthouse, where staff frequently find silverware mysteriously moved around.

furniture—and seemed about as far from scary as I could imagine a place to be.

I quickly found Linda, the volunteer I was seeking, sitting in what had probably been a formal dining room. She looked up from her book and greeted me with a warm smile. As soon as I explained the reason for my visit, Linda invited me to have a seat with her so she could tell me about Captain Joseph Willie Townsend, the lighthouse's primary ghostly resident. She described him as a bit of a prankster, but not a ghost she or any of the other staff had ever been afraid of.

"He was originally from Bristol, England," she said. "Captain Townsend lived here from 1901 until he died of consumption in one of the upstairs bedrooms in 1910." Consumption is an old-fashioned term for tuberculosis. "Because he died in winter when the ground was too frozen to dig a grave, the Captain couldn't be buried straight away, and his body had to be stored in the basement for several months." Some of the paranormal

Childrens' bedroom at Seul Choix Point Lighthouse.

investigators who have visited Seul Choix believe that might be why the captain's spirit remains "trapped" at the lighthouse.

Linda had her own ideas. She told me that the hauntings didn't really start until a couple of original pieces of furniture were brought up from storage, when the lighthouse was last restored in the 1990s. One of the pieces in question is the kitchen table.

"In England," Linda went on, "you set a table correctly by putting the knife and spoon on the left and the forks on the right." That's the opposite of the way we set a table here in the United States. "The Captain doesn't seem to like it when we set the table American style. We always find the silverware reversed, even though no one's been in the kitchen!" She laughed.

Like the other rooms, the kitchen is roped off so that visitors can look but not touch.

Numerous guests and most of the staff have smelled cigar smoke throughout the living quarters, even though no smoking is allowed in the building, and often there isn't anyone else around. Linda told me that, despite his health problems, Captain Townsend was a heavy cigar smoker, and it seems that even in death, he enjoys a good cigar.

In the mornings several volunteers have found a "crescent-shaped imprint" on the bedspread in the room they're pretty sure was the Captain's. "It looks like someone sat down right on the bed," Linda said. Some volunteers and visitors have reported seeing a man watching them from one of the windows, about half-way up the light tower—but no one was in the tower at the time.

Probably the eeriest of Linda's stories was one a guest told her. A woman was visiting the lighthouse sometime last year, and when she pulled in, she noticed a man wearing a heavy blue coat, walking across the yard to the lighthouse. Being friendly, she waved; he ignored her, but she didn't think that much of it. Like me, she went to the gift shop first, then went over to the lighthouse, looked around, and headed on her way. When she got home, the woman started doing some research on the lighthouse's history and realized that the man she'd seen in the yard was Captain Townsend! She contacted the lighthouse staff to tell them of her unusual encounter.

"Several people have seen a man wandering the grounds before," Linda told me, "but this was the first time someone positively identified the Captain, even though they didn't know who it was at the time."

I have to admit, hearing that gave me goose bumps!

In addition to Captain Townsend roaming the grounds, rearranging silverware, and ignoring no-smoking signs, volunteers have also found toys strewn all over the floor of the "children's bedroom" upstairs. Nothing had been out of place the night before, and, by all accounts, the lightkeeper's quarters had been locked up all night. Linda told me that she thinks the children's room might be haunted by the spirits of two of the little girls who grew up in the lighthouse. Although they grew up and moved away, both had recently passed on—and it was just about the time they died that the children's room became "active."

I thanked Linda for her time and went to have a look around for myself. Even though I had been told that a number of guests reported feeling the Captain's presence on the staircase, I didn't feel anything unusual. My camera continued to work too. I didn't smell cigar smoke or hear music. Even so, I appreciate antique furniture, so I enjoyed walking around the small house. And I appreciated the staff's sense of humor when I found the plastic Halloween skeleton hanging in an upstairs bedroom closet! I admit that it got me. I jumped.

When I came back downstairs, Linda let me step into the living room, which is normally roped off, so I could get a better picture of the antique organ, where the portraits of past light-keepers are on display. She also invited me to climb the tower.

The lighthouse at Seul Choix is a working light station and one of the few where visitors are allowed to climb the tower. Of course, no one lives in the lightkeeper's quarters today; the station is automated. A hundred years ago, however, the light was fueled by oil, which had to be carried by hand up to the light at the top of the 79-foot tower. Every two hours, the lightkeeper or his assistant hauled two heavy metal buckets up a very narrow spiral staircase.

Because I'd never been to a lighthouse before, I decided to go ahead and make the climb—despite my horrible fear of heights. As I climbed the narrow metal stairs, I marveled at how a man twice my size had made the same trip four or five times a night, carrying heavy buckets filled with oil. I stopped at the midway point to catch my breath and enjoy the view from one of the windows—and got the distinct feeling that I was being watched. But no one else was in the tower with me. Of course, it might have been my imagination; I'd spent the last 40 minutes listening to ghost stories. Although my nerves threatened to get the better of me (because of the height, not the ghosts), I made it to the top. The view of the lake was spectacular. That alone made the drive worthwhile.

The tower and lightkeeper's quarters are open to visitors from Memorial Day through mid-October. Guests are asked to make a small donation that goes to the Gulliver Historical Society to keep the lighthouse running. In addition to the lighthouse and gift shop, Seul Choix Point has a beautiful public beach, where I stopped to enjoy my lunch and take some more pictures before getting back on the road toward Marquette and the Landmark Inn.

CHAPTER 24

Landmark Inn
MARQUETTE

ALTHOUGH I HAD PLANNED most of the places I would
visit in advance, I had only made hotel reservations in a couple
of hotels along the way—namely, the ones that were reputed to
be haunted. The rest of the time, I sought out roadside motels
for simple accommodations and friendly, northern hospitality.
It was late enough in the season that there were few other tourists on the road, yet too early for hunters. Motel vacancies were
easy to find, which allowed me a flexible schedule to enjoy the
Upper Peninsula at my leisure. I tend to avoid the usual tourist attractions, but I did enjoy taking the time to hike through
state-owned forests and long stretches of Lake Superior's magnificent coastline. I met a number of wonderful people along

the way. One of them was a reference librarian in Marquette, who helped considerably with the research for this chapter. After all, librarians know everything (or so I've been told), and it is a fellow librarian who is said to haunt Marquette's historic Landmark Inn.

Originally called the Hotel Northland, the inn opened its doors in 1930. In its heyday, the Northland was host to A-list Hollywood talent, including Jimmy Stewart, Lee Remick, George C. Scott, Bud Abbot, and Lou Costello; and musicians, including Duke Ellington and Louis Armstrong. Aviation legend Amelia Earhart is also on the list of former guests of the prestigious Hotel Northland. The room in which she stayed is now called the Earhart Room. Likewise, the room occupied by Abbot and Costello bears the famous comedians' names.

Unfortunately, the hotel fell into disrepair during the 1970s and ultimately shut its doors in 1982. It remained closed until 1995 when Team Landmark, a company specializing in historic restoration, took on the monumental task of bringing the hotel back to its former splendor—and then some. The new owners had the idea to create a 62-room hotel that would feel like a bed-and-breakfast. Each room is uniquely decorated with antiques or replicas. Many of the rooms are themed, such as the Dandelion Cottage Room, with its white wicker furniture, or the North Woods Room, which is done up to look like a rustic log cabin—but still with all the amenities of a luxury hotel. Of special interest is the reputedly haunted Lilac Room on the hotel's sixth floor. The lilac room is called that because of the lilac-print wallpaper and lavender bedspread. (Unfortunately, I wasn't able to actually photograph the room when I visited because there was a guest staying there at the time—but I was able to sneak a peek inside when housekeeping went in to clean.)

I arrived in Marquette at about ten in the morning and headed straight to the Landmark Inn for brunch—and hopefully a few ghost stories. I have to admit, when I pulled up in front of the old, red-brick building, I didn't think I'd just arrived anywhere special. The exterior is anything *but* impressive. "Never judge a book by its cover," I reminded myself as I parked. And as soon as I stepped into the beautifully appointed lobby, I understood why the Landmark Inn is called the "jewel of downtown Marquette." The front lobby is everything you'd expect from an upscale hotel: white marble floors, dark wood-paneled walls, crystal chandeliers, and Oriental rugs.

I made my way to the main dining room but rather than being seated right away, I asked the hostess if she had a minute to talk. "I'm writing a book about haunted locations in Michigan," I explained, "and the Landmark Inn came up in my research into the Upper Peninsula's ghost stories."

She told me she was new at the hotel and hadn't seen or heard anything herself. "But everyone warns not to go up to the sixth floor alone, especially at night," she added with a laugh. "I don't know if should take them seriously or not. They might just be 'hazing' the new girl."

Good point.

The hostess sat me in the section of a waitress who had been there for a while, who could hopefully help with material for this chapter. My server was busy when I first sat down, so I put in my order and waited until she delivered my scrambled eggs with salmon and capers before asking about the sixth floor's ghosts. She was a little reticent at first—not everyone who asks about the hotel's haunted history takes it seriously—but as I told her about some of the other places I'd visited on my trip, she relaxed and promised to come back and talk as soon as she got another guest's food out.

"I've never seen anything myself—but I don't go up there either," she said when she returned to talk. "I had a customer one morning, a man, who complained about how loud the

The famous "Lavender Room" of the Landmark Inn.

guest in the room next to his was. He said he'd called the front desk several times to complain, but they didn't do anything. I had a minute, so walked over to the front desk to find out what was going on—we want our guests to be happy, and if someone isn't, we try to fix it. They checked the computer and said I must have gotten my customer's room number wrong, there was no one staying on either side of him. When I asked my customer to repeat his room number—and asked which room all the noise was coming from—I knew what the problem was. The noise was coming from the Lilac Room. I didn't want to tell him the room next to his was haunted, so I just suggested he ask for another room.

"I had another customer," she went on, lowering her voice just a little. "Another man. She," the Lilac Room's ghost, "doesn't like men very much. The first time he came down for breakfast, he commented about the blinds in his room. He'd drawn them before bed but was woken up in the morning by bright sun, because somehow the blinds had gotten opened in the middle of the night. I asked him what room he was in and he told me: the Lilac Room. I told him that if he wanted to, he could probably switch rooms, but he said it was no big deal. When he came down for breakfast the second morning, he said the same thing had happened. He drew the blinds before bed, but by morning, they'd mysteriously opened, letting in sun. The third night, he told me he *tied* the cord in place, so there was no way it could come loose in the middle of the night. But it did. In the morning the blinds were up again. He didn't know anything about our ghost, and I didn't tell him. He was checking out that day anyway."

There's a reason the Lilac Room's resident specter acts out more toward male guests than women who stay there: The ghost is said to be that of a lovelorn librarian who died of a broken heart in the 1930s. She was in her 30s and had never been married. Today, we might not think much of a 30-year-old woman who is single, especially if she has a career, but 70 years ago, women married and started families young. Few had careers outside the home. A woman in her 30s would find herself with few prospects for a husband, which meant not only loneliness, but social and financial insecurity as well. One can only imagine how happy the librarian must have been when she caught the eye—and heart—of a visiting crewman. He worked on one of the many iron ore freighters that regularly docked in Marquette. The city was, and still is, a major port town, with a bustling iron ore industry.

The librarian and her sailor courted, often meeting at what was then the Hotel Northland, and eventually planned to marry—after he returned from one last voyage across Lake Superior. But he never came back. His ship was caught in a storm and sank, taking all hands to the bottom of the lake. The librarian never recovered from her broken heart and soon passed away herself. Many believe she returned to the inn after her death to wait for her love on the sixth floor, where they used to meet. Some guests have reported seeing a "ghostly woman" standing in the hall, staring out the window at Lake Superior.

Front desk personnel report calls coming from the Lilac Room when there are no guests staying there. Guests have said they get calls in the middle of the night, but when they pick up the phone, no one is there. Many have reported having trouble getting their room keys to work—and again, the bulk of the problems are reported by male visitors to the hotel.

The front desk clerk I spoke to said that it wasn't unusual for guests to ask to change rooms, sometimes in the middle of the night. "A lot of guests tell us they feel like someone is watching them, even though no one's there. One man said he felt the bed sag, like his wife was getting into bed with him—but then he rolled over and realized she was still in the bathroom getting ready for bed."

On the other hand, the bartender I spoke to told me that while he knows some staff members refuse to go up to the sixth floor alone at night, he thinks they're just psyching themselves out. "It's dark up there at night, so it's easy to get freaked out, especially if you know the story." He told me that the only thing he found "weird" about the Lilac Room was the lavender color pallet. "No wonder guys don't like to stay there," he added.

Before I left, I asked the front desk manager if it would be all right to go up the sixth floor myself, as long as I promised to be unobtrusive. When I got up there, the housekeeping staff were making their rounds, and I talked to a few of the ladies about the Lilac Room. They all reported being familiar with the ghost, but not frightened by her—then again, all of the housekeepers I talked to were women.

Spotlight On: Orb Photos

There is a lot of debate over the phenomena of "orb" photos. Some people say that the only thing being captured in the images are flecks of dust, insects, or moisture in the air. Ghosthunters believe that the orbs are connected to spirit manifestation, although even among paranormal researchers, there is some debate on exactly what causes the orbs to appear in photographs. Occasionally, people even claim to see orbs with the naked eye, such as the encounter Margaret Perry told me she had while eating her dinner in the Fenton Hotel's dining room, or the children at the Whitney.

With the advent of digital cameras, capturing orb images has become easier than ever. Paranormal researchers—and weekend ghosthunters—no longer have to wait for film to be developed; images can be checked on location. I sat down with paranormal investigator Tracy Harrell and asked her to share some of her ghosthunting techniques, especially how she gets great orb photos—and how she knows they're really something supernatural and not just a fleck of dust in the air.

"Do you recommend any particular kind of camera?" I asked.

"I use a digital camera. Any camera with a flash will do; it doesn't have to be expensive. You can even get good results with your cell phone, as long as it has a flash."

"Any special tips for capturing orbs on camera?"

"It just takes some patience," she advised. "Sometimes you have to visit the same place more than once to capture something. It's best to go when it's dark out," she added. "Of course, it helps to go to a cemetery known for paranormal activity."

"What about trespassing laws?"

"Unless there are hours posted or there's a locked gate, most cemeteries don't actually close after dark," she told me. "Out in the country, most people don't care, and most older cemeteries only have rudimentary fences around them. If somebody does ask, we tell them we're out ghosthunting and that's pretty much the end of it. I look at it this way," she went on, "who would the police rather have out there, a bunch of kids or us? Besides when we're out, we're a pretty good deterrent to kids out getting drunk or whatever. We have cameras and we won't hesitate to take their photos to hand over to police."

Obviously, there are some well-known cemeteries that should be avoided at night, such as the Lakeville Cemetery that has unfortunately become very popular with teenaged miscreants. The most famous cemeteries often are patrolled by local police.

"But you don't have to go to a 'famous cemetery' to get good photos," Tracy assured me. Her favorite haunts are old country graveyards.

"I've always wondered," I said, "why is it better go out after dark and to use a flash? Is it that ghosts only come out at night?"

"No, not at all. Orbs tend to be milky or pearlescent. If I were to take a picture in this room, and there was an orb, it might not show up." We were sitting in a well-lit hotel lobby. "It's not that it wouldn't be there, we just wouldn't be able to see it. Dim the lights and we could probably catch an orb on camera."

Tracy had some additional advice to pass on. "Always carry back-up batteries, even if your batteries are brand new. Always document your trip. I keep a journal where I record the location, date, time, weather, if there were a lot of mosquitoes out. That way, if you start going through your photos and discover a few really great shots, you can go back to your notes to rule out any obvious 'natural' reasons for the orbs. That's why I always take multiple shots in rapid succession of the same place. If I get an orb or some other anomaly, like a mist or a streak of light that only shows up in one of the pictures, chances are it was just dust or a bug. It's also a good idea to take out more than one camera."

"Do you have any favorite cemeteries?" I asked her.

"Two that I can think of. There's one on Herbst Road, in Brighton, and one in Highland where I almost always get good photos. You should come along with us some time," she added.

Now there's one invitation I can't wait to accept!

CHAPTER 25

Calumet Theatre
CALUMET

THE KEWEENAW PENINSULA juts out approximately 40 miles into Lake Superior, making it the northernmost stretch of land in the Great Lake State. Not exactly a day trip for those of us who live in the southern part of Michigan, but it was more than worth the couple of hours it took me to get there from Marquette. The site of one of the most extensive deposits of copper in the world, Keweenaw's economy was once based solely on the mining industry. Later, lumber production took over as a major industry, but now, at the turn of the 21st century, the peninsula's economy centers around the tourist trade and jobs created by the two colleges that call Keweenaw home: the Michigan Technological University—or simply Michigan Tech—and

Findlandia University. I scheduled an entire day in Keweenaw so I would have plenty of time to see the sights. In addition to the town of Calumet, there are a number of "ghost towns," mostly abandoned copper-mining towns that are open to the public (although caution is advised when visiting them).

But before I went sightseeing, I had work to do! I had heard about the Calumet Theatre from an acquaintance who said he had attended a classical music concert there and had a "strange experience." Or, more accurately, the pianist had, and later told audience members about it. During the performance, the pianist "got the strangest look on her face," my acquaintance told me. She wasn't just getting into the music, "she was staring at something offstage." She explained later that she'd seen a "ghostly mist." Although the gentleman I spoke to hadn't seen anything, other audience members claimed to have seen it too. I was skeptical but certainly intrigued.

According to local legend, the Calumet Theatre is haunted by the late actress Madame Helena Modjeska (October 12, 1840–April 8, 1909), who even today is considered to be one of Poland's greatest stage actresses. She came to the United States in 1876 with her husband, Charles Bozenta Chlapowski, and although the couple settled in Southern California, Madame Modjeska toured all over the country. She appeared not only on stages in cities like New York and Chicago but also in rural communities as well, although by all accounts, the Calumet Theatre was a prestigious opera house in its day.

The town, which was originally called Red Jacket, was settled in 1864 by workers from the Calumet and Hecla Mining Company, one of the largest copper-mining operations in the United States at the time. In its heyday, Red Jacket was at the very heart of the peninsula's copper-mining region and enjoyed tremendous financial and cultural prosperity. The Red Jacket Opera House opened its doors on March 20, 1900, and when the village changed its name to Calumet in 1929, the opera house became the Calumet Theatre.

Calumet's downtown historic district consists of more than 60 buildings that have all been restored to look like they did at the turn of the last century. Anyone who appreciates old architecture or regional history will enjoy a stroll through downtown Calumet. The main attraction is definitely the beautiful Calumet Theatre, where Madame Modjeska appeared in a production of William Shakespeare's *The Taming of the Shrew* almost a hundred years ago. She wasn't the only star whose name graced the theater's marquee at the turn of the last century. Other famous performers included Lillian Russell, John Philip Sousa, Sarah Bernhardt, Douglas Fairbanks Sr., Lon Chaney Sr., James O'Neill, and Frank Morgan. The theater still hosts productions, but in addition to professional shows and concerts, it is also the home of the Calumet High School's theater, band, and choir events.

The theater welcomes visitors year-round, offering guided tours during the summer months between 11 a.m. and 2 p.m., and allowing for self-guided tours between 2 p.m. and 5 p.m. During the rest of the year, guests are welcome to have a look around on their own during regular box office hours. Because my trip up north was taken during the autumn, I'd called ahead and made an appointment with the theater's executive director, Laura Miller, who agreed to make some time to talk to me. She was on the phone when I arrived, so I asked the ladies working in the box office if they had ever had any encounters with the theater's resident ghosts.

"Oh yes," one of them said. "Practically everyone who works here has." Employees and patrons alike report seeing shadows or misty apparitions like the one I'd heard about. People often hear voices in the theater, even when no one else is working or run into "cold spots," a common phenomenon in reportedly haunted buildings.

"Nothing scary," the other lady in the ticket booth added. "Madame Modjeska just likes to make her presence known." It seemed like I'd definitely come to the right place for ghost stories!

In addition to the famous Polish actress, there are several other specters reported to haunt the Calumet Theatre—at least according to the Internet. According to several websites that I found, the theater is the site of two murders. The first victim was supposedly a young girl named Elanda Rowe, whom local legend tells us was murdered "somewhere on the theater grounds." The second incident involves an unnamed gentleman who was supposedly murdered in the theater in 1903. Both ghosts are said to "scream at night," but no one I talked to has ever heard any screaming, and I wasn't able to find any factual evidence to back up either story. It seems like these reports are nothing but urban legends.

What I was able to verify was that in 1913, the Calumet Theatre was used as a temporary morgue for the bodies of 73 people, most of them children, who had died during the "Italian Hall Tragedy" on Christmas Eve of that year. Some 500 striking copper-mine workers and their families were attending a Christmas Eve party on the second floor of the Italian Hall, which was located down the street from the Calumet Theatre. In the middle of the festivities, someone was heard to holler "fire!" and in the ensuing panic, people rushed for the single staircase leading to the ground floor. Many tripped and fell on the steep steps and were either trampled to death or suffocated as other people rushed over top of them, fleeing to safety. To this day, no one knows who called out the dire, and patently false, warning, but when rescue workers cleared the bodies, they were removed to the nearby Red Jacket Opera House, now the Calumet Theatre. In 1941, folk singer Woody Guthrie wrote a song called "1913 Massacre" about the tragedy. Many of the miners blamed the

Haunted second balcony of the Calumet Theatre.

incident on the company bosses, alleging that not only were they responsible for the cry of "fire," but that they had the doors of the hall locked. Although there remains no solid evidence to back up the allegation, the Italian Hall Tragedy is the subject of many books and a recent documentary.

Paranormal investigators often say that when people die sudden or traumatic deaths, their spirits have a tendency to get "stuck" here on earth and may attach themselves to places like the Calumet Theatre, where the bodies were laid out for some time after the tragedy at the Italian Hall. A number of psychic and paranormal investigators have visited Calumet and have recorded evidence of ghostly activity in the area of the theater that was used as a temporary morgue and also in the small memorial park that was erected in honor of the victims on the site where the Italian Hall once stood.

As soon as she was off the phone, Laura apologized for the delay and invited me back to her office so we could talk. She was very interested in the book I was writing and had personally accompanied a number of the paranormal teams that had investigated the Calumet Theatre. "They always get EVP and EMF readings on the stage," she told me.

Another place where there seems to be a lot of spirit activity is the second balcony, which for safety reasons is closed to visitors unless they are accompanied by a staff member. Several people have told Laura that they've heard "voices speaking in theater jargon," and have seen movement in the second balcony even when no one should be there. "We keep the doors locked," she added.

Laura went on to tell me what had happened to one of the lighting technicians one night after the theater had hosted a performance by the Calumet High School drama department. "There's always a lot of activity after the high school has a performance here," she added. On that particular night, the theater's tech and drama department heads were cleaning up after the performance, and both swore they saw someone dart across the second balcony. Assuming it was just one of the students up there "exploring" where they shouldn't be, they called for the teenager to come down. No one answered. When the men went up to investigate, they found the doors locked and no one in sight. It was enough to convince them both that the theater was indeed haunted.

Laura told me that a few years ago she was visited by a woman from California who claimed to be psychic. According to her, "there are a lot of disquieted spirits" in the second balcony.

Even so, Laura repeated what the lady in the box office had said about not feeling uneasy in the theater, even when she's there all alone at night doing paperwork. "I work part-time for a couple of businesses in the historic district," she explained. "It's easy to let your imagination get the better of you when you're alone in some hundred-year-old building with all the lights turned off. This is the only place I've never felt uncomfortable."

That was good to know, especially as Laura went on to tell me about some of her personal experiences with Madame Modjeska. She asked me if I'd noticed the portrait of Madame Modjeska hanging in the front lobby. Yes, I had.

"When I first started here, everyone warned me that Madame Modjeska doesn't like her portrait moved," said Laura. "Whenever someone does, something always happens to them. Never anything big," she added, telling me how one person who moved Madame Modjeska's portrait tripped on the steps and twisted her ankle. It might just have been a coincidence, but the staff always blames little mishaps like that on Madame Modjeska's ghost. Heedless of the warning, Laura moved the actress's portrait during the Christmas season one year to put up a wreath. Shortly thereafter, she was working late in the box office by herself. "I was trying to get a ticket to print and it just wouldn't come out. Finally, on the third try, it printed." But instead of printing like it should have, the words "ghost writer" were written on the ticket, along with a picture of a Snoopy dog. Now, the printer *is* equipped to print words, but nowhere in its programming is there an image of Snoopy.

Why Snoopy? Laura showed me her keychain: it's a bronze Snoopy, her favorite *Peanuts* character. She thinks it was Madame Modjeska making herself known. "Just saying 'hello.'" But since that was the worst thing that happened to Laura after moving the portrait, the rest of the staff have decided she's the only one allowed to touch the picture. Apparently, Madame Modjeska likes Laura.

After we talked for a while, Laura showed me around the theater. When we went back stage she showed me the place where most people have reported seeing Madame Modjeska during performances. In fact, during one such performance in 1958, the famous actress's spirit was first seen by a young woman performing on the stage. The story the young actress told is that she forgot her lines and that Madame Modjeska appeared to her and prompted her, getting her back on cue. No one else saw Madame Modjeska—or any other ghostly apparition—during that night's performance, but ever since that time countless visitors, actors, and staff members have seen the Polish diva. Typically, she appears in a purple gown.

Laura gave me a quick tour of the rest of the theater and let me take some photographs, but had to apologize for not having time to show me the second balcony. There was a performance that night, and she had to get back to work. That was all right, as I already had a lot to write about. I thanked her again for her time and headed out with a lot to think about.

In addition to my visit to Calumet that day, I toured the Eagle Harbor Lighthouse, which, according to several Internet sources, is also haunted. Unfortunately, when I arrived I couldn't find anyone who had ever had any unusual experiences or who even knew the lighthouse was supposed to be the site of ghostly activity. Lesson learned: call ahead before trekking out into the middle of nowhere! Still, I didn't consider it a wasted trip. The lighthouse is rich in maritime history, and my kindly tour guide suggested I take the scenic route up Brockway Mountain Drive before heading back down to Marquette. It was a perfect day for a drive, so I took him up on the suggestion and found the view of the lake and surrounding countryside to be absolutely breathtaking. It was definitely worth the 40 or so minutes it took me out of my way.

CHAPTER 26

Whitefish Point Lighthouse and Shipwreck Museum
PARADISE

I BELIEVE IN SERENDIPITY, that is, that things happen for a reason. I'm certain it was exactly that kind of good luck that led me to Whitefish Point.

The Point's lighthouse wasn't on the list of places I intended to visit on my weeklong trek, but it turned into the best stop I had up north. I wouldn't have ended up there if it weren't for several random choices and a little bit of following my gut. I had some time to kill at the end of the week, so when I reached M-123, driving back from Calumet, I decided to head north instead of south. I had seen a couple of signs for Tahquamenon Falls, so

I thought, "What the heck?" and decided to check them out. I remembered seeing pamphlets for the falls when I stopped in St. Ignace, almost a week before. The falls are supposed to be spectacular.

But I wouldn't know; I never made it that far!

M-123 runs through the Sault Ste. Marie State Forest and along the shore of Lake Superior, where it follows the shoreline of Whitefish Bay and cuts through the town of Paradise. The sun was beginning to set when I pulled into town, so I decided to find a place to stay for the night and drive out to the falls in the morning. I had quite a few choices for overnight accommodations: hotels, motels, cabins. I opted for the Paradise Inn for no other reason than it was the most traditional-looking hotel in sight—although being walking distance from a restaurant helped tip the scales in its favor.

When I handed over my driver's license, the gal behind the desk grinned; she'd grown up less than five miles from where I live. "So what brings you all the way up here?" she asked, as she handed it back. I really didn't look like the average tourist; Paradise is popular with hunters, birdwatchers, hikers, and fisherman. I looked a bit more like a hippie in my long silk skirt and blouse.

"I'm writing a book about haunted locations around the state," I explained.

She smiled again. "Oh, so you're here for Whitefish Point." It wasn't a question.

"No," I admitted. "But I'd love to hear more about it."

"You have *got* to go up to the lighthouse. We get those paranormal people out here all the time. A couple of years ago, those guys from the science fiction channel came out. They stayed right here!"

So much for my plans of taking a whole day just to relax and sightsee!

As soon as I got settled into my room, I booted up my laptop and searched out the Whitefish Point Lighthouse website,
shipwreckmuseum.com, to get directions and some more information. It looked like the lighthouse was right up the road, less
than a 20-minute drive, which meant I could sleep in, since
they didn't open until 10 a.m.

Whitefish Point juts out a few miles into the eastern end of
Lake Superior, but it is an important turning point for shipping
traffic in and out of the lake. It also marks the eastern end of
an infamous 80-mile stretch of shoreline known as "Shipwreck
Coast." Whitefish Point itself is sometimes called a "Graveyard
of Ships," as nearly half of the ships that have been claimed by
Lake Superior's unforgiving waters were lost within the vicinity
of the Point. Little wonder the light station, established in 1849,
is the oldest working lighthouse on Lake Superior.

Although I was familiar with the tragic story of the *Edmund
Fitzgerald*, a freighter that went down in Lake Superior on
November 10, 1975, I hadn't realized that the ship was lost less
than 20 miles off Whitefish Point. All 29 crewmembers were
lost; the story was put to music by Gordon Lightfoot in 1976.
The Great Lakes Shipwreck Historical Society recovered the
Fitzgerald's bronze bell in 1995, and it remains on exhibit in the
Shipwreck Museum at Whitefish Point.

I arrived at my destination early the next morning and
noticed a group of people hauling their gear out of the former
Coast Guard Crew Quarters, now a fully operational bed-and-
breakfast. I thought little of them or the amount of gear they
were hauling out of the building—I've been known to pack a
lot too!—and made my way up to the museum. There was a
$15 admission charge that covered admittance to the museum,
lighthouse keeper's quarters, and boathouse, as well as to a small
theater where visitors could view a short film on the recovery of
artifacts from the *Edmund Fitzgerald*.

I hung near the back of the line so I could talk to the cashier without holding anybody up, and I have to admit I was surprised to *find* a line of people at 10 a.m. on a Monday morning late in September. As soon as I told the cashier about the book I was writing, she offered to call over to the Crew Quarters and see if someone could come talk to me. "Beth, our housekeeper, is the resident expert on ghosts around here!"

That sounded good to me. In the meantime, I paid the admission and had a look around the museum. When Beth arrived, we chatted a bit. She was warm and welcoming and she took me over to meet that group of people I'd seen leaving the Crew Quarters when I first arrived. Turns out they weren't just tourists; they were members of the Motor City Ghost Hunters, paranormal investigators based out of metro-Detroit. The group had just finished up a weekend-long investigation of Whitefish Point. Beth told them about my book and introduced me to team leader and founder, John, lead investigator and "sensitive," Chass, as well as Tom, Kellie, and several other team members. Despite having been up late the night before, they were more than happy to talk to me about their experiences at Whitefish Point. John gave me his card and suggested I use their website (motorcityghosthunters.com) as a further resource. He graciously invited me to email him if I had any questions. Like I said, serendipity. Whitefish Point wasn't on my list of places to visit, and if I'd turned right instead of left, I never would have ended up there. I made some great contacts and had a fantastic tour of the site, compliments of Beth.

That weekend had been the Motor City Ghost Hunters' fourth visit to Whitefish Point. They told me it was one of their favorite places to visit because every time they come up, they find something new. "It's like spirits are attracted to the place," John said. Both he and Beth speculated that spirits might be attracted to the lighthouse's beacon. It would seem logical that sailors would hone in on the light. But it's not just the ghosts of mariners lost to Lake Superior's icy waves that visitors have spotted at Whitefish Point. Guests staying overnight at the Crew Quarters have reported seeing apparitions of men dressed in Coast Guard uniforms. Doors in the old building are said to open and shut by themselves, and numerous visitors have reported being touched in the middle of the night—especially ladies staying in the downstairs bedrooms.

After chatting with the Ghost Hunters for a while, Beth offered to show me around. I was delighted to have a tour guide. The first place we went was the Crew Quarters, which aren't normally open to the public since there could be guests staying over, but after talking to the Ghost Hunters, I really wanted to see the building. Beth told me as we walked that her ghosts are "real pranksters." She calls her favorite ghost "Stinky" because of the strong cigar or pipe smell people report smelling in certain rooms of the Crew Quarters. The first time she smelled it, Beth was certain a guest had been smoking in one of the bathrooms, but no one even *had* a cigar or a pipe. She suspects that "Stinky" was one of the Coast Guard crewmembers who lived there almost 50 years ago. Beth spoke affectionately of the ghost. In fact, I was surprised by how many people I met during my trip up north genuinely enjoyed the presence of the spirits reported to reside where they work.

"Stinky steals keys," Beth cautioned me, as we entered the building (I immediately made sure I knew where mine were!). "There's one set that I *still* haven't found. I'd like them back, please!" she added, just a little louder, not talking to me at all. "Sometimes things get moved around in the kitchen. I, or one of the guests, will put something on the table or the counter, and the next time we see it, it's in a drawer on the other side of the room, even though no one touched it or saw it move."

Beth led the way to the downstairs bedrooms where several

guests have reported being touched in the middle of the night. "The guy down here really seems to like the ladies," she said. "One woman told me she thought her husband had come to bed, because she felt his side of the bed sag and then she felt a hand on her back. But when she rolled over, she saw that her husband was still in the bathroom brushing his teeth."

After touring the Crew Quarters, Beth walked with me over to the lighthouse keeper's quarters. Although the lighthouse has seen many different keepers throughout the years, one of the most memorable was Captain Robert Carlson, who lived at Whitefish Point from 1903 until 1931. During much of that time, his granddaughter Bertha Endress Rollo (1910–2007) also lived there. During the 1980s, Mrs. Rollo worked with the historical society at Whitefish Point to restore the lighthouse to its former elegance. She donated much of the furniture and artwork that had belonged to her grandfather for the exhibits in the light-keeper's quarters. There are many pictures of Mrs. Rollo as a young girl throughout the old family quarters in the lighthouse. As Beth pointed out, she is always smiling, so if perhaps her spirit has returned to its childhood home, there is little to be afraid of.

However, Beth said there was one room in the lighthouse that made her very uncomfortable. They call it the children's room; it's one of the upstairs bedrooms and is decorated with a crib, children's toys, and an old baby doll lying in a wooden cradle near the center of the room. "A lot of people say they see a child staring down at them from that window," Beth pointed to the window in question. "It could be a little girl or a little boy, but I think it's a little girl." She said she believed that the girl died in the room, although she has yet to uncover any concrete proof to support her theory. Certainly a lot of families lived in the lighthouse over the years. "There's just something about this room that I don't like," she said, again.

When Beth asked me if I felt it too, I had to confess that the room did make me a little uneasy, but then again, when you listen to ghost stories, it's easy to let your imagination run away with you. Or maybe it was just the antique doll in the room that gave me the willies; I've never liked old dolls. Beth told me that one morning she came in to discover that the cradle the doll rests in had mysteriously broken overnight. No one could figure out what had happened to make the wood crack like it did.

Finally, Beth took me over to the Shipwreck Museum. She wanted to show me the exhibit about the SS Myron, which sank in 1919 off the coast of Whitefish Point. The bodies of the 17 crewmen who perished in the wreck washed ashore some months later; they are some of the very few men who have died on Lake Superior whose bodies were ever recovered. The men are buried in the Mission Hills Cemetery in Bay Mills Township, one of the many cemeteries I visited on my trek across the Upper Peninsula. Beth told me that she always feels drawn to the Myron's exhibit, as though the spirits of those who died onboard are still clinging to the artifacts from the sunken ship. For my part, I felt a sense of sadness around all of the relics that had been recovered from the ships that went down near Whitefish Point. I suspect that that was just my own reaction to the tragic deaths of so many young men.

Ghostly phenomena has also been reported by guests and observed by members of the Motor City Ghost Hunters along the beach near Whitefish Point, where there is a memorial for the crewmen of the Edmund Fitzgerald. Many people have reported seeing apparitions or feeling as if they're being watched. A few people have even reported being touched while they walked along the beach.

I had such a great time at Whitefish Point that I'm planning a trip back in the spring. After all, I never did get to visit Tahquamenon Falls! In addition to the falls, the famous Pictured Rocks are located just a little farther down the shore from Whitefish Point. I'd also like to check out the Whitefish Point Bird Observatory in warmer weather. The observatory is a 44-acre nature preserve that is a regular stop-over for migratory birds. Some of the species spotted there include eagles, hawks, falcons, owls, as well as geese and ducks. And when I come back, I know just where I'm going to stay—the Crew Quarters at Whitefish Point. After my stay at the Blue Pelican (see Chapter 28), I think I'm up for another night in a haunted inn.

Spotlight On: Ouija Boards

According to the website for the Museum of Talking Boards (a.k.a. Ouija boards) "modern spiritualism" began in Hydesville, New York, in 1848, when sisters Kate and Margaret Fox (ages 12 and 15, respectively) claimed to have contacted the spirit of a dead salesman. The method they used for communing with their spirit friend is known as "rapping"—that is, getting the spirit to rap or knock on a table during a séance. Messages could be spelled out this way by asking a spirit to knock once for "A" twice for "B," and so on. Although Margaret later claimed the whole thing was just a hoax and even went so far as to demonstrate their methods to the public, the idea of speaking to the dead had already spread like wildfire across not only the United States, but also Great Britain and other European countries.

Since the dawn of human history, the idea of spirits has fascinated people, and many have sought ways to communicate with those who have passed over to "the other side." Even after the Fox sisters were debunked, other mediums (called such because they acted as intermediaries between the living and the dead) continued to refine their methods of communicating with the deceased. Automatic writing replaced rapping; a pencil was attached to a small basket, and the medium would place his or her fingertips on it and allow the spirit to take over and write out their message. Automatic writing is still practiced by psychics today.

Eventually, the heart-shaped planchette, or "little plank," which was used to point to letters already printed out on a board, replaced the basket and pencil. This, of course, was the original Ouija board. The first patent for a commercially produced "talking board" was filed on May 28, 1890; it lists Elijah J. Bond as the inventor.

I came into contact with my first Ouija board when I was a teenager. Some of my friends were amazed by the thing, others terrified. I have to admit, I was skeptical. Maybe that's why I never got any meaningful messages out of it. Nothing bad happened either, although certainly books and the Internet abound with stories of people who have had terrible, supposedly supernatural, experiences after playing with a Ouija board. Two of the people I talked to while writing this book, Lynn Hay, of Main Street Antiques in Holly, and Julia Chapp, who owns the Sweet Dreams Inn Victorian Bed-and-Breakfast, in Bay Port, don't allow Ouija boards to be brought into their businesses.

I haven't met up with any professional ghosthunters who use Ouija boards to communicate with spirits, but they do use some of the other methods used by early Spiritualist mediums. It is not uncommon for ghosthunters to ask spirits to knock or make a noise to indicate their presence during an investigation. In addition, some ghosthunters use a flashlight that has been lightly "tampered with," so that the connection between the bulb and battery is tenuous. Usually, it's just a matter of unscrewing the head so that it sits loosely on the base. Spirits are then asked to turn the flashlight on and off to let investigators know they are present and willing to communicate. Obviously, there is some question as to the accuracy of this method, but it's something to keep in mind if you decide to book a room at a known haunted hotel.

Northern
Michigan

Central Lake
  Blue Pelican Inn
Petoskey
  City Park Grill
  The Noggin Room Pub and Stafford's Perry Hotel
Traverse City
  Mission Table at Bowers Harbor Inn

CHAPTER 27

Mission Table at Bowers Harbor Inn

TRAVERSE CITY

ALTHOUGH PROBABLY BEST KNOWN for its wineries and annual Cherry Festival, Michigan's Traverse Bay area is also the home of the Mission Table (formerly called the Bowers Harbor Inn). Located 20 minutes north of Traverse City on the coast of the Mission Point Peninsula, Mission Table was the first stop on my ghosthunting journey. I'd never sought out and visited reportedly haunted hotels or restaurants before, so I was a little nervous, unsure how my questions about specters would be received by staff, other guests, and owners. I was pleasantly surprised by the warm welcome I got at the Mission Table.

The drive up from Detroit was a long but pleasant one, and despite technical issues with my GPS, I had no difficultly locating the summer-retreat-turned-fine-dining-restaurant using the directions from their website (missiontable.net) as my only guide. The big blue building sits on the peninsula's main road, and though it is sheltered amongst the pine trees, it's not hard to miss. As I drove around to the parking lot, which looks out over a vineyard, I tried to remember as much as I could of the story of Genevieve Stickney, the Mission Table's resident spectral inhabitant.

Genevieve and her husband J.W. Stickney, then an up-and-coming Chicago businessman, purchased the property in the late 1800s. At the time, the property consisted of an old farmhouse with a small orchard of fruit trees, and was one of only a handful of homesteads on the peninsula. While J.W. built his million-dollar-plus lumber-and-steel empire, Genevieve went to work building her own successful, home-based business, making jams, jellies, and brandy. Eventually, the couple tore down the old farmhouse and built the mansion that stands on the property today, which they used as a summer retreat.

Sadly, a story that should have been happily-ever-after ended in betrayal and heartbreak. As she aged, Genevieve became increasingly overweight, which resulted not only in a decline in her health, but increasing depression and emotional insecurity. One of the employees at the restaurant told me that at one point, Genevieve removed all of the mirrors on the property, presumably because she didn't want to look at herself any more. Genevieve is often described by historians of the Inn as "bitter" and "jealous." It was during this period of physical and emotional decline that the Stickneys installed an elevator between the first and second floors, because Genevieve was no longer able to climb the stairs. J.W. also hired a young nurse to assist his ailing wife, but it turned out the nurse was doing more to help J.W. than Genevieve. When J.W. passed away, Genevieve discovered that J.W. and the nurse had been carrying on an illicit affair behind her back for years. J.W. left his entire fortune to the nurse; Genevieve was left with only the house. She fell into a deep depression and eventually hanged herself from the rafters in the elevator.

Since Genevieve's death, the property has changed hands several times, with little if any reports of ghostly phenomena until 1959, when Jim and Fern Bryant purchased and renovated the old house and began converting it into a restaurant. Since then, there have been many sightings of Genevieve and even a few of J.W.

In 2006 John Carlson and Greg Lobdell, natives of Mission Point Peninsula, purchased the property and changed the name to the Mission Table. Carlson and Lobdell have worked closely with the Grand Traverse Regional Land Conservancy and Michigan Historic Preservation Network to preserve and protect the historic estate. In addition, Carlson and Lobdell instated a menu that includes local produce and spotlights locally brewed beer and wine from local wineries.

Arriving a little before three in the afternoon, I found the Mission Table Restaurant wasn't open yet, but the Jolly Pumpkin, a cozy little pub located at the rear of the main building, was serving lunch. I only wished I didn't have several more hours of driving ahead of me after I left Traverse City; I would have loved to have tried one of the local beers with my lunch. After ordering, I rather sheepishly gave my preplanned speech to my server: "My name's Helen, and I'm here because I'm writing a book about haunted places in Michigan . . . " I'd barely gotten the word "haunted" out of my mouth when my waitress's eyes lit up a bit and she smiled.

"I don't actually believe in ghosts," she told me quietly, "but this place is *definitely* haunted!" She promised she'd be back to talk to me as soon as she cashed out her other table. Well, that had gone better than I'd feared! (The Mission Table does have a whole page on their website dedicated to Genevieve's story, but you never really know how people are going to react when you start asking them about ghosts.)

When my waitress returned, she told me that she'd spent a lot of time at Bowers Harbor Inn when she was younger. "My family used to bring me in here all the time, but I never saw or heard anything until I started working here a few months ago." She was careful to explain that everything she'd experienced could be explained as something *other* than Genevieve playing tricks. Lights flickering, even a beer tap going on by itself, could probably be explained away as "just one of those things."

But we both agreed that while flickering lights could be caused by a loose wire, beer taps don't usually just open up and start pouring on their own (she'd lost several pints of beer before she got it shut off again; it wasn't just a trickle). I've worked in restaurants myself and have poured beer from taps; they're not hard to pull, but they don't just fall open without help. Still, a loose beer tap isn't proof positive of Genevieve Stickney's after-life presence in her home.

While I finished my lunch, my server went to find another waitress, Terri, who had been there longer and could tell me a lot more about Genevieve. Terri was getting ready for dinner service in the Mission Table restaurant, and I was invited to walk around upstairs before going over to talk to her.

The Jolly Pumpkin and Mission Table are connected through a short series of halls and stairs, and customers are welcome to go up and have a look around. I eagerly climbed the stairs and walked down a narrow hallway into the main building, the home Genevieve had shared with her husband, J.W., a hundred years ago. Looking around, it was apparent that the owners had gone to great lengths to preserve much of the turn-of-the-19th-century charm, and it was easy to imagine what it must have been like for the Stickneys, during the happier days of their marriage, spending summers in this big, beautiful house on the lakeshore.

Even knowing the whole story I didn't feel anything especially ominous as I walked around upstairs—until I ducked into the ladies' room to change the batteries in my camera, which was starting to act up (most likely that had more to do with me than any ghosts!). As soon as I opened the ladies' room door, I immediately felt . . . *something*. Not quite a chill, but some sort of presence. Of course, I shrugged it off at once. Ever the skeptic, I figured it was my own mind playing tricks on me; after all, there I was prowling around all alone in an old, reputedly haunted building. So, convinced I was spooking myself, I switched out my camera's batteries and went downstairs to find Terri. She was in the main dining room setting up for an early dinner reservation, but more than happy to take a few minutes to talk to me.

Terri had been at the Mission Table "from the start," since the new owners took over in 2006—and from the very beginning, she'd been aware of Genevieve's presence in the old building. It started at one of their first staff meetings; the entire staff was assembled in the dining room, not far from where we were standing. "I was sitting right over there," she pointed to the far corner. "We were going over the menu and we were getting to taste everything when suddenly I felt a chill." Terri told me she initially shrugged it off, but then the woman sitting next to her asked "do you feel that?" She'd felt the same icy chill.

Of course, it's an old building—it could just have been a draft, right?

Terri didn't think so, and by the time we were done talking, I was inclined to think there might be something to Genevieve's story too.

Terri told me that on another occasion, she and another waitress were standing upstairs near an ornate gold mirror that hangs in the hallway, surrounded by old photographs. (According to several histories online, this mirror was purchased by the Stickneys because it seems to make people looking into it appear slimmer.) Terri and her coworker were standing on opposite sides of the mirror, but no one was in front of it. She describes what they both saw reflected in the mirror as "an aura" or a misty apparition. It passed across the mirror and vanished. Neither woman would have believed what they'd seen if someone else hadn't seen it too.

The next story Terri told me was about the ladies' room upstairs—the one I felt the presence in. (I hadn't mentioned my experience to her.) Apparently, the ladies' room is one of Genevieve's favorite haunts. One night when Terri was changing clothes after work in the ladies' room upstairs, she heard a loud rattling at the door of the outer room. (The ladies' lounge upstairs has two rooms—the lounge area and the restroom itself.). She shrugged it off, but upon exiting, an irate customer accused her of holding the door shut, preventing her from entering. Terri was nowhere near the door when the customer was trying to open it—and the door doesn't have a lock. She said Genevieve has held the door shut on several people.

Terri told me that on another occasion, when she was serving a large party, one of the guests asked about the restaurant's haunted history, adding quite firmly that she doesn't believe in ghosts. Terri smiled and offered to tell her a few of her personal stories if the guest wanted to hear them, as soon as she had a minute. As dinner progressed into dessert, Terri served this particular woman a dish of frozen yogurt. The dish was cold, the yogurt was cold . . . and a moment after Terri set it in front of her customer, the dish shattered (no one was hurt). Terri jokingly "tisked" her customer, saying that was what she got for saying she didn't believe in ghosts. Then a thought occurred to her.

"Are you a nurse?" Terri asked her customer.

Puzzled by the odd question, the guest confirmed that yes, she was. Why?

Terri told her Genevieve's story. Apparently, the only time Genevieve is known to get at all nasty is when it comes to nurses. Little wonder, given her husband's infidelity.

Terri did tell me that she's never felt uncomfortable working in the old haunted restaurant; she tells Genevieve "good night" every day when she leaves work. "Gennie's more of a prankster than anything else," Terri expressed firmly. "She likes to play with the lights and the sound system." On any number of occasions, management has turned everything off for the night and gone upstairs to do the end-of-the-day paperwork, only to come back down later to find the lights and music back on, even though no one else was in the building and the doors were securely locked. Terri also told me that when the owners were renovating the landscaping a while back, workers dug up all sorts of jam and jelly jars—Genevieve had gotten quite eccentric in her later years and had taken to burying things around the property, apparently fearing people were trying to steal from her. Terri brought up the fact that it must have gotten awfully lonely out there in Genevieve's day—the peninsula wasn't always the tourist attraction it is today.

As we were talking about Genevieve, both Terri and I experienced goose bumps and would have sworn there was someone watching us. Proof of ghosts? Probably not, but it was enough to make me wonder.

Spotlight On: Ghosthunting Equipment for the Weekend Ghosthunter

Professional ghosthunters, like the folks from the Motor City Ghost Hunters, use some pretty sophisticated—and expensive— equipment. Chances are that's more of an investment than the average person wants to make. The good news is that the weekend ghosthunter can get by—and still get good results—with just a few ghosthunting tools.

A good-quality digital camera is an absolute must, and the greater the resolution (the more pixels) the better. I use the camera that I bought a couple of years ago for vacations. It has the added bonus of being small enough to fit easily in my purse. I use rechargeable batteries—but always carry a backup set (except for that one time at the Baldwin Theatre, the one time I needed them!). It is commonly reported that batteries die and electronics stop working in haunted places.

A second indispensable piece of equipment, according to everyone I spoke to, is a digital recorder. Most digital recorders are small and inexpensive. All of the ones I looked at had a record time of several hours.

Digital recorders are used to pick up EVPs, or electronic voice phenomena. Paranormal investigators frequently seem to record sounds and even voices on electronic devices, even when no sounds or voices were heard by the team members themselves during the investigation. Many paranormal teams post these recordings on their websites, allowing visitors to decide for themselves whether the "voices" caught on tape are real or just white noise.

A digital camera and digital recorder were the only pieces of equipment I took with me on my adventures around the state, and I really only used my digital recorder a few times. I left it on all night when I stayed at the Blue Pelican—but if anyone was there, they didn't feel like talking to me.

Probably the next most popular ghosthunting device is an EMF detector, which is used to detect electromagnetic fields. The theory is that where there are ghosts, the electromagnetic fields "spike." Other things can cause electromagnetic fields to jump too, such as outlets and major appliances. So you need to have an idea of what's in the area before jumping to conclusions. Natural and man-made (not paranormal) electromagnetic fields can cause people to have that same "eerie feeling" so many people get when they believe there are spirits nearby. Bearing in mind that you get what you pay for, weekend ghosthunters can purchase a decent EMF meter for $30–50 from most larger hardware stores. More expensive models start at $100.

A couple of the paranormal investigators I spoke to recommend using a 35mm camera, preferably loaded with black-and-white film, as a secondary source for ghostly images. If you're going out with a friend, it might be interesting to compare images taken with a digital camera and the good old-fashioned way with film.

If you're more serious—or as you become more serious—you can add additional equipment to your ghosthunting arsenal. Full-spectrum digital video cameras are popular, as are night vision or infrared camcorders.

It has been suggested to also document your adventures with pen and paper—or maybe start a ghosthunting journal or blog.

CHAPTER 28

Blue Pelican Inn
CENTRAL LAKE

I LEFT THE MISSION TABLE late in the afternoon and headed for Central Lake and the Blue Pelican Inn, where I had a room reserved for the night. Central Lake is a small northern Michigan town surrounded largely by farmland. It is located in what is known as the "chain of lakes," a system of small lakes in the Traverse Bay area that has become a popular destination for skiers, campers, hunters, and fishermen from across the Great Lake Sate. When I arrived at the Blue Pelican, I found the dining room filled with people who had been out on the golf course all afternoon and were just coming in for a bite to eat.

Ron, the manager on duty, told me that it was a fairly typical Tuesday night. The Blue Pelican's dining room is busy almost year-round, but, as it happened, I was the only overnight guest at the Inn. As soon as I told Ron that I was writing a book about ghosts, he asked me if I'd like to stay in Room Number One, or the Cherry Room, which is one of the Blue Pelican's supposedly most haunted rooms. I was more than up for it!

It was only after my dinner that I discovered I was the only guest at the inn and I would be staying overnight alone. None of the staff remains on the premises after dinner service is over. Was I scared? Not really. It gave me a great opportunity to do a little ghosthunting of my own. If I did happen to hear or see something, I would know with certainty that it wasn't the house-keeper or manager making nightly rounds.

The Blue Pelican has gone by a variety of names over the years. Built in 1924 by local stonemasons Art Carpenter, Joe Blakely, and Jack Garrison, it was designed as a small hotel with the original structure featuring 22 guest rooms and a dining room. Currently, there are only seven guest bedrooms, each decorated with lovely antiques, hand-stitched quilts, and antique furniture. Ron told me I was free to wander into any of the other rooms I wanted to and mentioned that several employees and customers had told him they'd seen faces peering out the upstairs bedrooms when no one was staying in the rooms in question. One worker swore that he saw a face peering out at him through a window of a room that was boarded up at the time, due to renovation. Many guests have reported seeing the ghosts of the two people who are known to have died at the Blue Pelican.

During the Inn's early years, it was managed by Mr. and Mrs. Emmons Gill. Ron told me that Mrs. Gill died on the property in one of the upstairs bedrooms in the 1950s. It was shortly after her death that employees and guests began seeing ghosts at the inn. A few years ago, a guest was able to supply the inn's current owners, Chris and Merrie Corbett, with a photograph of

Mrs. Gill, which sits in the wine case in the front lobby. Looking at Mrs. Gill's smiling face, it was difficult to be frightened of her ghost—if indeed she does haunt the place.

But Mrs. Gill wasn't the first person to die at the Blue Pelican Inn. The first documented death occurred in the 1930s when the young daughter of the inn's manager tripped on the hem of her dress while climbing down from a small second-story balcony and fell to her death. She was sneaking off to elope with her fiancé. Many guests have seen her wandering the upstairs hallway wearing a white dress, perhaps the wedding dress she never got to wear in life. Others have reported only a white cloud of mist, but they say they are sure it was a woman—or at least her spirit.

In addition to Mrs. Gill and the young bride, there are reports of the ghost of a little girl who has been seen looking out of an attic dormer. Upon investigation of the property's history, the Corbetts discovered that the inn had been used as a temporary school when the original Central Lake School burned down many years ago. Ron thought the little girl might have been one of the students who died in the fire. Perhaps she wanted to be with her classmates and followed them in death to the new school, but when they left, she lingered on behind.

Other guests have reported seeing a little girl in the basement of the inn.

Heading up the stairs to my room for the first time, I got a sense of . . . something about halfway up the steps. It was the sort of something that you can't put a finger on but makes you think maybe the ghost stories are real. I stopped for a moment and looked around, but no one was watching me—no one was upstairs at all. The upstairs hallway is long, straight, and relatively narrow, with guest rooms along both sides. At one end of the hall is the door that leads to the balcony where the young bride lost her life in the 1930s—that door is securely locked.

"Rose Room" at the Blue Pelican Inn (the room I stayed in when I visited).

I quickly found my room and noticed that the doors have glass knobs, like the kind in the house I grew up in. The locks all require metal keys to open, not the card keys found at most hotels. After settling in, I explored the rest of the guest rooms, taking both my digital camera and digital audio recorder along with me. I didn't catch any strange sounds or orbs, but I did get that odd feeling again in Room Number Two, which is the other room with a lot of reported spectral activity.

Or maybe the ghost stories had gotten to me.

The Inn has been visited by a number of paranormal investigators over the years, including teenaged filmmaker, Cruce Grammatico. I discovered Cruce's video series, "Michigan Uncovered" on YouTube after I came home from my trip up north. Cruce's "Blue Pelican Investigation" is now available for viewing on the inn's website. After watching it, I contacted the young filmmaker, who agreed to talk to me about his team's overnight stay in Central Lake. He said that once the employees and other guests began to clear out, the inn took on an "eerie" feeling. "The team felt nervous as they began their investigation, starting in the upstairs bedrooms," he told me.

The first thing that struck me when I was watching the video for the first time was that Cruce and his team got an EMF meter spike at exactly the same spot on the staircase as I got my first sense that maybe the place really was haunted. Proof of ghosts? Probably not, but definitely interesting. EMF meters measure electromagnetic fields and are used by paranormal investigators to detect and track both explainable energy sources (such as power lines and household appliances) as well as fluctuations that cannot be easily explained. According to the paranormal researchers I talked to, a "spike" between 2.0 and 7.0 is considered indicative of spirit presence.

After investigating the upstairs bedrooms, Cruce told me he took his team into the basement banquet rooms. "I would be lying if I said it felt normal," he told me. "We started to do an EVP session and immediately started hearing footsteps above us, but we were completely alone in the building."

EVP stands for electronic voice phenomena—all you need is a digital or tape recorder and a lot of patience. I tried a little EVP experiment myself when I stayed overnight at the Blue Pelican, leaving my digital recorder on all night while I slept, but the only thing I caught was my own snoring.

Cruce reports a much more exciting EVP session in which they heard a young boy say, "I'm here." According to owner Chris Bartlett, "You don't see much, but you hear a lot."

My only notable experience at the Blue Pelican Inn occurred just as I was getting ready for bed. It was late and everyone had gone home for the night. I'd also had enough time to poke around and get a good feel for the natural sounds of an old building—the house I grew up in is about as old as the Blue Pelican. I was just about to tuck in for the night when I heard a loud *click*. I recognized it immediately as the sound of one of the door handles turning, and it sounded like it was coming from one of the rooms down on the other end of the hall.

Except all of the doors were already open.

And I was alone at the Inn.

I left early the next morning, heading out long before any staff members arrived for lunch service. I had breakfast down the street and walked around downtown Central Lake for a while, enjoying a warm early autumn morning. Everyone I talked to knew that they lived and worked just down the street from a haunted inn, but no one seemed bothered by the ghost stories.

Spotlight On: Electromagnetic Fields and Ghosts

An electromagnetic field (or EMF) is simply a field of energy produced by electrically charged objects. Human beings emit electromagnetic fields, as does the earth itself. So do electrical appliances, both large and small. EMF detectors measure the amount of electromagnetic energy in a given area—typically a very small area.

Paranormal investigators are interested in electromagnetic fields for a couple of reasons, but mainly use EMF meters to seek out and make note of man-made sources of electromagnetic energy, such as power outlets, electrical wiring, computer monitors, televisions, and household appliances. Why? Because many people are sensitive to electromagnetic energy. For those people, coming into contact with an electromagnetic field causes feelings of paranoia, like they're not alone, even in an empty room. This is the cause of that "eerie feeling" so many people report in supposedly haunted locations. Even people who are not particularly sensitive to electromagnetic energy experience these same feelings if they come into contact with a strong enough field. So, the first thing ghosthunters have to do when they arrive at a location to conduct an investigation is rule out natural or logical reasons for seemingly ghostly phenomena, including electromagnetic fields.

Although some people believe that spirits can also affect electromagnetic fields and cause them to fluctuate radically, causing a spike in the EMF meter's readout, this isn't necessarily the case. The truth is that no one knows what ghosts are made up of and what effect they have on the environment—or if they even exist at all. What an EMF meter will do is help investigators become better acquainted with their environment.

The first thing to do after purchasing an EMF meter is to become familiar with how it works. Simply practice by seeking out electromagnetic fields around your home in places you would expect to find them, such as around electrical outlets, in the kitchen, laundry room, and so on. Then walk to an area where you wouldn't expect to find much electromagnetic energy, and note the difference in the reading. Always take this kind of base reading when entering a new environment. Also, remember that EMF meters are very sensitive to movement, so it's important to walk around *slowly*. Sudden movements will skew a meter's reading and you'll end up with false readings. For this reason, regardless of what they show us on television, EMF meters are not at all useful for "chasing ghosts." At best, an unexplained spike in a reading can tell researchers that *something* is going on around them—what that something is will probably always be up for debate.

CHAPTER 29

The Noggin Room Pub and Stafford's Perry Hotel

PETOSKEY

I DECIDED TO TAKE MY HUSBAND with me to Petoskey on Michigan's northwest shore—on my last ghosthunting adventure. The village was settled in 1879 and is named after the state's stone, a type of fossilized coral that is found in abundance there. It took my husband and me about five hours to drive from our suburban home up to Petoskey, but we couldn't have asked for a nicer day or a better place to visit. Petoskey is a quiet little town that still looks very much like it did back at the turn of the last century. It is a favorite destination for vacationers year-round, especially those looking to escape the city and get out into nature—or people like me, looking for a good ghost story or two. On the way to Petoskey, we passed the Boyne Mountain ski area—not being a skier myself, I hadn't realized how close northern Michigan's favorite ski resort was to our destination.

Our only planned stop was the City Park Grill, but my husband seemed to be having some issues with the GPS—or maybe it was having issues (I'm sure that's the story *he'll* tell). When I saw a sign for the Stafford's Perry Hotel, I told him to park the car.

"I read something about this place online," I fibbed.

The whole story was that the first time I drove up through the area, I stopped at a different Stafford's Hotel, the Bay View—there are several properties under the Stafford name—and got some odd looks when I started asking about ghosts. It wasn't until later that I discovered I was at the wrong Stafford's Hotel. Since we were right in front of the Perry Hotel—and apparently hopelessly lost—I decided to go in.

My husband dutifully parked the car along one of the side streets across from the hotel, and we made our way around to the side entrance, where a short staircase led us down into the Noggin Room. I began by approaching the bartender on duty.

"We're haunted all right," he told me. "But I'm not really the person to ask." He took us over to the front desk because he thought the person who worked there knew more about ghosts than he did.

The lady on duty told us the same thing as the bartender. The hotel was definitely haunted, especially room number 310, but she didn't know much about it, just that the night auditor claimed to see stuff all the time.

"We have a book in the lobby you could read," she offered, helpfully.

Right. I decided to go back to the Noggin Room and try talking to another staff member instead. My husband and I had already decided we were going to stay for lunch anyway, so we sat down in the cozy, pub-like dining room to look over the menu. When a young waitress named Lauren came over to get our drink order, I explained the real reason for our visit.

"I don't suppose you've ever heard or seen anything?" I asked, hopefully.

I was starting to get discouraged by that point, although I wasn't about to admit to my husband that we may have just driven six hours for nothing. I had sort of sprung the trip on him at the last minute because I didn't want to make the drive alone if I didn't have to.

Lauren told me the same thing as everyone else. Yes, they were haunted, but, no, she didn't really know the details.

"But if you want to wait around a little, the night bartender, Michael, knows everything about this place," she said.

I looked at my husband, who just shrugged. It was already almost two o'clock. So we, or rather, I, decided we'd have a nice leisurely lunch, complete with appetizers and desert. When the calamari arrived, we both decided we'd made the right call. Ghosts or not, the food was worth sticking around for.

A little before three o'clock, Lauren brought Michael over and introduced us. She told him I was looking for ghost stories about the hotel.

"We definitely have a few of those," Michael assured me, as he sat down with us. "I won't bore you with stuff you've probably already read; most of those predate me anyway," he said.

I took out my notepad and started taking notes, as Michael explained that the story he was about to tell was really about a certain "artifact"—but that to tell it right, he was going to have to start several days before he and some of his coworkers found it.

"It was February of 2010," he began, "during our Winter Blues Festival. We had balloons tied to all the chairs. I finished my shift, left work, and was headed out of town for the night. I'm driving along, and I get this frantic phone call from my manager. He told me he'd just turned off the last light and was

Third-floor library at Stafford's Perry Hotel—where staff members found the mysterious red book.

getting ready to lock up for the night, when suddenly he heard this loud "pop" and then the pitter-patter of little feet running across the dining room floor. Sure enough, when he looked around, he saw that one of the balloons had popped. He was totally freaked out. I just laughed. I told him the ghosts were just saying 'hi' and not to worry about it. He said, 'I don't want them to say hi, I don't even want to know about them!' He was a total skeptic."

Michael explained that there were several ghosts who are supposed to haunt the hotel. Upstairs on the third floor a woman named Doris is believed to haunt the library, although room 310 also seems to see a lot of supposedly paranormal activity. Besides Doris, there is a ghostly custodian named Keith, and a little girl who plays in the restaurant and occasionally roams the halls. Perhaps she was responsible for popping the balloon that freaked Michael's manager out so badly.

Michael told us that one of his coworkers had actually had a much closer encounter with the little girl. She told him that she noticed a little girl sitting in a chair in the hall, kicking her heels.

"She thought the little girl must be a guest," Michael said, "and so she stopped to ask if she was all right, but the girl didn't answer. She started back down the hall but glanced over her shoulder just a couple of seconds later, and the chair was empty. There was no sign of the little girl anywhere."

Okay, that would be much more likely to freak me out than a popped balloon!

"The incident with the balloon happened on a Tuesday," Michael continued. "The next night I was back at work. It was Lauren's first night," he added, glancing up at our waitress.

She nodded. It was a fairly slow weekday afternoon, and she'd stuck around to listen to Michael's ghost stories too.

"So it was me and her and a couple other wait staff," Michael continued, adding that the same manager who had called him the previous night after the balloon mysteriously popped was with them as well. "The place was closed and were all sitting up at the bar cashing out, and I was talking to them about the hotel's ghosts. Lauren was a little freaked out."

She nodded again. "Everybody's heard stories about this place, but working here . . . ?" she shrugged. "I wasn't really sure what to expect when I first started."

"I told her that the best thing to do was to just walk out into the restaurant and introduce herself," Michael said.

"I felt a little silly about walking into the middle of the restaurant and saying 'hi' to thin air," Lauren told us.

"I said I'd be right behind her," said Michael. "So she walks into the middle of the room and I'm with her; so is the other waitress who had closed with us and our manager. Well, we get out to about here," he nodded to a spot not too far from where we were sitting, "and all of a sudden something comes flying out from that area there." Michael pointed to what looked like a storage area nearby. "Lauren and the other waitress screamed,

I started looking around trying to figure out what it was, and our manager was already back by the kitchen! It only took me a couple of seconds to find what had come flying out. It was one of the nozzles from the pop dispenser. We have two, and we take them off at night to soak them in a pitcher of water."

I nodded; I'd worked in enough restaurants to know that routine. If the nozzles aren't soaked nightly, they tend to clog up because the pop syrup builds up.

"The thing was," Michael went on, "when I found the nozzle on the floor, it was dry. We walked over and checked the pitcher of water the girls had put the nozzles into earlier, and there was only one in it. We knew the nozzle that had come flying at us had to have been one of the ones they'd put in to soak. It should have been wet."

I was definitely intrigued. Stafford's Perry Hotel doesn't advertise their ghost stories the way most of the other properties I had been to over the last few months did; all I'd been able to glean from the Internet were a few tantalizing hints that there might be something interesting going on here. It seemed I was right.

"The next few days were pretty quiet," Michael told us. "But that Saturday there were about eight of us sitting around after work. There were a bunch of new staff members, and we were talking about some of the weird stuff that had been going on all week, and one of the other staff members mentions the library. So we all decided to go up there and have a look around. We got up there and the manager notices a lump in the rug. We lifted up the rug and there was this huge wet spot. In the middle of the wet spot was a dry ring. In the middle of *that* was this little red book. So I picked it up and the book was dry. It wasn't an old book; it was printed in 1984 and it looked like it was in pretty good condition."

Michael got out his cell phone and showed us a picture of a small dark red book. The title was clear: *You Can Live Forever in Paradise on Earth*. He said that the picture he had pulled up to show me wasn't actually taken on the night the book was found, because at the time, no one thought it was that unusual.

"The only 'odd' thing was that the book wasn't marked with the hotel's stamp," said Michael, "but we just figured it must belong to a guest, that maybe somebody's kid was playing a prank or something, hiding one of his parents' books under the rug. I put the book on the shelf over the fireplace, with a set of big blue encyclopedias. Then I kind of jokingly said something like, 'Hey, Doris, if you wanted us to have this, just leave it here, and I'll come back and get it tomorrow.' We all laughed a little and then went home."

Michael told me that the next day, the book was gone. They didn't really think much of it, however. Whoever it belonged to must have gone into the library, found it, and taken it home.

The next few months passed uneventfully, but then in May, Michael said he was hanging out at a friend's house after work when one of the waitresses called him, "freaking out."

"She kept saying, 'It's back, it's back!'" he told us. "I asked her, 'What's back?' She sent me this picture." He flipped through his phone to pull up a photo of the little red book wedged into a water pitcher. "The story I got," Michael explained, "was that her and the manager (the same manager who has been in all the stories about the little red book) were sitting up by the bar talking after work. The woman who called me said she felt something behind her. She and the manager both looked and saw this dark mist—which isn't that unusual, a lot of people have seen it down here."

I had to say that someone who works in a haunted building would call seeing a dark mist floating across the room "nothing unusual."

Michael laughed and went on with his story. "After they saw the mist, they decided it was a good time to finish up and go home. They were just getting the last of their work done when they turned back to the bar and saw the book. That's when they called me, just totally freaking out."

Michael said that after they took the book out of the pitcher, they noticed first that the book was only damp, so it couldn't have been sitting in the water pitcher unnoticed for any length of time, or it would have been soaked. They also noticed that there was a hole through the "o" in "you."

"They laid the book on a paper towel and put it behind the blender, out of sight," Michael continued. "When they came back in the next day, the book was gone. Now, the only people who knew about it besides them were the two front desk guys, who said they didn't touch it, and me, and I wasn't here. This place is locked up at night, so it's not like a guest could have come down and somehow found it. We had no explanation for why or how it went missing."

He added that one of the front desk guys told him that he'd come down to the restaurant around 6 a.m., to get a cup of coffee before going home, and he didn't remember seeing the book.

Now, by this time, Michael explained, he was starting to wonder if maybe someone was pulling a prank. After all, the same manager who claimed not to want anything to do with the ghosts had been there both times this little red book was found. *He* noticed the lump in the rug, and *he* was there when they found the book in the pitcher. Was that too much of a coincidence, or were the ghosts trying to make a believer out of a skeptic?

That summer passed peacefully, but on October 15, one of the business partners called Michael into the office and asked him to have a seat.

"And he opens up his desk drawer, and there's the little red book," Michael told us. "He'd heard stories about the book circulating among the staff and wanted to know if the book he'd found was *the* little red book everyone was talking about. I looked at it. It was bent, from when someone—or maybe something—had shoved it into the water pitcher, and there was the hole. I asked him where in the world he'd found it."

The man told Michael he found the book in the dumpster, sitting right on top of some white trash bags. The hotel only uses clear or black bags. They decided that if it was a hoax, it was an extremely elaborate one, and if it wasn't . . . well. Maybe it was easier to blame it on an ordinary human prankster.

The book remains in the business partner's desk for safe-keeping.

Before he left us, Michael told us about the ghost of a former custodian, a man named Keith, who haunts the second floor. The story goes that Keith loved the hotel, even though he often got stuck with the kind of grunt jobs nobody else wanted. Once, he even got accidently locked out of the building while cleaning windows on the second floor. I was sure the story was going to end badly—but a guest noticed Keith up there and he was let back in, no harm done.

Sometime after that, Keith was said to have remarked to one of the managers about how he would always take care of the place, because he was so grateful to them for giving him a job when nobody else would. I didn't get Keith's back story, just that whatever it was, he had said that working at the hotel had really given him a new lease on life.

A week or so after remarking that he would "always" take care of the hotel, Keith passed away. After that, it seemed as if windows were frequently—and mysteriously—found open on the second floor. A guest even caught what appeared to be an image of a ghostly figure outside a second-floor guest room window. Michael had a copy of it on his phone and showed me. It was difficult to tell what the image was, but it was certainly unusual.

If you stop by the Noggin Room when Michael is working, you might want to ask him to show you the photos he showed us. Some of them were pretty convincing.

CHAPTER 30

City Park Grill
PETOSKEY

AFTER MY HUSBAND AND I LEFT the Noggin Room, we went up to the third floor of the hotel, and I took a couple of photos of the library, and then we walked around a little outside. The Perry Hotel overlooks the bay, and it was a beautiful day. My husband put a few more coins in the meter while I stood looking out over the water, admiring the view. One of the waitresses from the Noggin Room came out to have a cigarette and joined me.

"You're the lady writing about the ghosts, right?" she asked. I smiled. "That's me."

"Well, you know where you really ought to go, since you're in town, is the City Park Grill."

I almost laughed. That was where we were supposed to have ended up. "How do we get there?" "Just go down the street, through the park, and make a left." She pointed. The City Park Grill was hardly a quarter of a mile from where we were standing.

"You should also check out the Mitchel Street Pub," the wait-ress advised me. "I hear it's pretty haunted too."

Armed with two good leads and knowing I had only one chapter left to write, my husband and I set off. Since it was the closest place—and because I was fascinated with the bar's his-tory—we set off toward the City Park Grill first.

The pub was originally constructed in 1875 by Alanso McCarty as a men's-only billiard hall, serving fine cigars, wine, and liquor to local clientele. In 1888, Frank J. Gruclich pur-chased the billiard hall, adding food to the menu and chang-ing the name from McCarthy Hall to the Annex. At the time, it was adjacent to the Cushman Hotel. Gruclich had a patio built into the east side of the building, and inside he added a stately, 32-foot, solid mahogany bar. That bar remains to this day.

Nine years later, in 1897, Gruclich passed away, and Frank Fotchman became the new owner of the business. Frank expanded the business, buying up the land just east of the patio, putting in a bowling alley in the basement, and opening up the Grill Café, in July of 1910. Shortly thereafter, and on into the 1920s, one of his regular summer customers was Ernest Hemingway. The Annex bar mentioned in Hemingway's short story "Gentleman of the World" is indeed the Annex bar in Petoskey.

But it isn't Hemingway's ghost who is said to haunt the City Park Grill; it is the spirit of Frank Fotchman whom employees and customers alike claim to see—or more often hear. Local story has it that Frank hanged himself in the basement in 1932. No one knows why, but most say that Frank poured his heart and

Frank's portrait and newspaper clippings on the wall of the City Park Grill.

soul into the business, and maybe that's why so many people believe that he is still there to this day.

My husband and I walked in and I asked the hostess if there happened to be anyone around who could give us a couple of minutes to talk about Frank's ghost. She didn't seem particularly fazed by the request and went to find her manager, who "can probably tell you more than me," she said.

A few minutes later, the assistant manager, Matt, came out to greet us. He was intrigued by the idea of *Ghosthunting Michigan*.

"I just wish I had more I could tell you," he said, explaining that he had only worked at the City Park Grill for a couple of years.

"You have to have heard something in two years," I replied.

"There's the usual stuff, glasses falling off bar shelves and breaking, stuff seeming to move all on its own—things that might be nothing. There was this one time, though," he admitted. "I was working late with a couple of other people. We'd just closed up and locked the doors, and one of the guys I was working with thought he saw someone passed out, probably drunk, in the hallway." He nodded toward the long hall that my husband

and I had seen when we first came in. "It happens once in a while," Matt explained. "Anyway, we went back to wake the guy up and see if he was able to walk home, or if maybe he was staying at the hotel, or did he need a cab or whatever—only there wasn't anybody there. The front door was locked," he repeated. "We looked all over the bar, but couldn't find any sign of any customers. That's the only time I've ever had anything like that happen."

According to Matt, for most of the employees at the City Park Grill, it's the basement that makes them the most uncomfortable. Of course, it's hard to say whether that's because Frank's ghost still lingers or because everyone in town knows that's where he killed himself. But Matt described the basement as "pretty eerie."

"One day I was up here working by myself, and I swear I heard footsteps coming up from the basement." He showed us the door that leads to the basement on the other side of the dining room. "I opened it up and looked down—no one was there. I shut the door again and tried to go back to work. I'm not the only person who hears weird sounds coming from the basement once in a while."

Matt called over one of the waitresses and asked her if she had ever seen or heard anything unusual.

"The chair," she told me.

"The chair?"

"I was working closing one night. I was out here cleaning up, and the cook was in the kitchen. I swept, wiped down all the tables, and pushed the chairs in, just like every night. Then I had to go into the back for something, I don't remember what now. But when I came back to the dining room, there was this one chair pulled out, like someone had been sitting in it. I didn't really think much of it at the time," she admitted. "I just pushed it back in and finished up what I had to do in back. I came back up for something else—and the chair was pulled back out again. No one else had been out in the dining room, and the front door was locked. I stayed in the back until it was time to go home."

That would definitely have been enough to make me not want to be alone in the dining room either.

"There's one other story I remember someone telling me," Matt went on. "One of the bartenders told me he'd seen this little girl, like poking her head out from around the corner. He thought it looked a little strange, so he went to check it out. He said there was no one there; it was like the kid had just vanished."

If we hadn't had to get back on the road, I would have stayed to have a drink at the same bar where literary giant Hemingway once sat. And even though I'm not typically a beer drinker, I probably would have sampled Short's Brewery's "Hangin' Frank's," a pale ale named after Frank Fotchman. Although Short's operates its own pub in Bellaire, where the brewery is located, Short's beers can be found in several other cities and bars, including, of course, the City Park Grill, whose famous former owner was the inspiration for the beer Short's labels their "contraversiALE."

Instead, I thanked Matt and his staff for their time, took a couple of photographs, and my husband and I walked back to our car. We're definitely going to head back up to Petoskey sometime—or at least I will.

Spotlight On: Mackinac Island

Earlier in the year, I visited Mackinac Island, which is supposed to be one of the most haunted places in the state of Michigan. It seemed little wonder, given the age of the settlement. Even before Europeans arrived in 1634, the island was inhabited by members of the Ojibwa tribe, who considered the island to be the home of the "Gitche Manitou," or "Great Spirit." Unfortunately, while I had a great stay, the first two days I was there, the only people I was able to talk to were seasonal employees who either didn't know anything about the island's hauntings, or who didn't want to talk about it. On my last day, I decided to get up early, walk into town, and talk to a few of the locals. They were much more helpful.

The island is a popular summer destination for Michiganders, most of whom come to get away from the city for a few hours and indulge in Mackinac's most famous commodity: fudge. I could easily have gained ten pounds in one weekend alone if it weren't for all the walking I did, and my family would not have let me back in the door if I hadn't brought home a half pound each of everybody's favorite flavors. Mackinac is accessible only by boat or small plane, and there are no motor vehicles permitted on the island. To get around, visitors walk, rent bicycles, or take a horse-drawn cab. Horses can also be rented for exploring the island's many beaches and trails. While many people only go for a day trip, I visited in the off season and got a great deal on my hotel room, proving that it doesn't have to be as expensive of a weekend getaway as a friend had warned me it would be. I stayed at the Mission Point Resort, which is so well known for its ghosts that the resort was visited by the crew of the SyFy channel's "Ghost Hunters," in March 2011.

There are a lot of ghost stories circulating about the Mission Point Resort, which was originally built in 1825 by Christian missionaries

William and Amanda Ferry. Many guests report seeing the spirits of children who died on the property during a tuberculosis outbreak in the mission's early days. The infected children were quarantined in a cellar to protect the rest of the population; few survived. The resort's most famous spirit, however, is probably Harvey, a lovelorn man who jumped to his death from one of the cliffs behind the resort after his girlfriend broke off their relationship. Harvey's room was located in what is now staff quarters, but guests have reported seeing him wandering other parts of the hotel as well. In fact, I mentioned this project to an acquaintance when I returned from my trip to Mackinac, and he said a friend of his worked a summer at Mission Point a few years ago and declared the place "totally freaky."

When I visited the Baldwin Theatre, administrative manager Vonnie Miller told me a story about her experiences on Mackinac Island. When Vonnie was a teenager, she visited the island and snuck out one night after curfew. She couldn't recall exactly where in town she'd been, just that she looked up to see a man standing under a light, watching her. She was sure she was going to get caught—only a second later, the man was gone. Vonnie told me that after she saw that, she hurried back to where she was supposed to be staying.

I did a little nighttime investigating at Fort Mackinac when I was on the island. The British built the fort in 1780, and it was the scene of two battles during the war of 1812. Allegedly, the spirits of many long-dead soldiers still patrol the fields behind the fort at night, perhaps not realizing that they're dead and the war long over. I didn't see any ghosts, just a few bats . . . but it was kind of dark, and maybe I was just a little bit nervous being up there all by myself at eleven o'clock at night. I'd just taken the walking ghost tour.

In addition to the walking tour, sponsored by the bookstore in downtown Mackinac, the Mission Point Resort has started a yearly tradition of hosting a "haunted weekend" in September. Guests booked into the special package are given the opportunity to participate in a real paranormal investigation and decide for themselves if the place is actually haunted.

When I go back for another visit, I'm not only going to schedule more time to explore the rest of the island, but I'll probably stay at the Cloghaun Inn, a little bed-and-breakfast in the heart of town. According to the owner of the coffee shop where I ate breakfast on my last day, the bed-and-breakfast is "definitely haunted." I stopped by to talk to the owners before I left, but they were in the middle of breakfast service, and I had to catch my ferry home. Not that I'm *looking* for an excuse to go back or anything. . . .

Michigan Haunted Road Trip Travel Guide

AMERICA'S
HAUNTED ROAD TRIP

Visiting the Haunted Sites

Below is the contact information for all the places I visited while researching this book.

SOUTHEASTERN MICHIGAN

The Whitney
4421 Woodward Avenue
Detroit, MI 48201
(313) 832-5700
Website: thewhitney.com
Hours of operation: Lunch served Tuesday–Friday, 11:30 a.m.–2 p.m.;
   Dinner served Tuesday–Saturday, 5–10 p.m.;
   Sunday Brunch: 11 a.m.–2:30 p.m.

Marlow's Chill and Grill
23307 Telegraph Road
Brownstown, MI 48314
(734) 362-0900
No website
Hours of operation: Open seven days a week for lunch and dinner

Camp Ticonderoga
5725 Rochester Road
Troy, MI 48058
(248) 828-2825
Website: campticonderoga.com
Hours of operation: Monday–Thursday, 11 a.m.–10 p.m.;
   Friday and Saturday, 11 a.m.–11 p.m.; Sunday, 11 a.m.–9 p.m.

Baldwin Theatre
415 S. Lafayette Avenue
Royal Oak, MI 48067
(248) 541-6430

Website: stagecrafters.org
Box office hours: Monday–Friday, 10 a.m.–4 p.m.

Bone Head's BBQ
10256 Willis Rd.
Willis, MI 48191
(734) 461-9250
Website: boneheadsinc.com
Hours of operation: Tuesday–Thursday, 11 a.m.–9 p.m.;
   Friday and Saturday, 11 a.m.–10 p.m.; Sunday, noon–8 p.m.

Battle Alley Arcade Antiques Mall
108 Battle Alley
Holly, MI 48442
(248) 634-8800
Website: battlealleyarcade.com
Hours of operation: Monday–Saturday, 10:30 a.m.–5:50 p.m.;
   Sunday, noon–5 p.m.

Main Street Antiques
118 S. Saginaw
Holly, MI 48442
(248) 634-1800
Website: mainstreetantiquesinholly.com
Hours of operation: Monday–Saturday, 10 a.m.–5 p.m.;
   Sunday, 11 a.m.–5 p.m.

Holly Hotel
110 Battle Alley
Holly, MI 48442
(248) 634-5208
Website: hollyhotel.com
Hours of operation: Victorian High Tea served Monday–Saturday,
   2–5 p.m.; Dinner served daily, 4–10 p.m.
   Sunday Brunch served 10:30 a.m.–2:30 p.m.
*All menus change daily; reservations are required for Sunday
   brunch and strongly encouraged for dinner and tea*

Fenton Hotel Tavern
302 N. Leroy Street
Fenton, MI 48430
(810) 750-9563
Website: fentonhotel.com
Hours of operation: Monday–Thursday, 4–10 p.m.;
    Friday, 4–11 p.m.; Sunday, 3–8 p.m.

THUMB AREA

Castaways Food and Spirits
4058 Hunt Road
Lapeer, MI 48446
(810) 245-8500
Website: castawaysrestaurant.com
Hours of operation: Monday–Friday, 11 a.m.–9 p.m.;
    Saturday, 11 a.m.–midnight; Sunday, noon–8 p.m.

Time on Main Street Euro Café
69394 N. Main Street
Richmond, MI 48062
(586) 430-1731
Website: timeonmaineurocafe.com
Hours of operation: Monday–Saturday, 8 a.m.–9 p.m.;
    Sunday, 9 a.m.–7 p.m.

Boomers Tavern
35005 Bordman Road
Memphis, MI 48041
(810) 392-3125
No website

Forester Township Cemetery
The cemetery is located on Lakeshore Road, just north of Forester Road in
    Forester Township, MI.

Sweet Dreams Inn Victorian Bed & Breakfast
9695 Cedar Street
Bay Port, MI 48720
(586) 863-2920 or (586) 322-6170
Website: myspace.com/sweetdreamsinn
Please call ahead if you're going to be in the area and want to stop by.

WESTERN MICHIGAN

Henderson Castle
100 Monroe Street
Kalamazoo, MI, 49006
(269) 344-1827
Website: hendersoncastle.com
Hours of operation: Henderson Castle's dining room is open to the public
  seven days a week.
  Breakfast: 8–10 a.m.
  Lunch: 11:30 a.m.–2 p.m.
  Dinner: 5:30 p.m.–8:30 p.m.
  Seasonal menus change daily

The National House Inn
102 Parkview
Marshall, MI 19068
(269) 781-7374
Website: nationalhouseinn.com
Please call ahead if you're going to be in the area and want to stop by.

Regent Theatre
211 Trowbridge Street
Allegan, MI 49010
(269) 673-2737
Website: cityofallegan.org/regent.php
Hours of operation: Monday–Friday, shows start at 7 p.m.
  Saturday and Sunday, movies start at 2 p.m.
  The Regent has a single screen and shows first-run movies.

Grill House Restaurant

1071 32nd Street
Allegan, MI 49010
(269) 686-9192
Website: grillhouse.net
Hours of operation: Monday–Thursday, 11 a.m.–9 p.m.
  (grilling begins at 4:30 p.m.)
  Friday and Saturday, 11 a.m.–10 p.m. (grilling begins at 4:30 p.m.)
  Sunday, 11 a.m.–8 p.m. (grilling available all day)

Kirby House Restaurant

2 Washington Street
Grand Haven, MI 49417
(616) 846-3200
Website: thegilmorecollection.com/kirby.php
Hours of operation: Lunch service begins at 11:30 a.m. seven days a week

Dee-Lite Bar & Grill

24 Washington Street
Grand Haven, MI 49417
(616) 844-5055
Website: harborrestaurants.com/deelite/index.htm
Hours of operation: Monday–Thursday, 6 a.m.–9:30 p.m.;
  Friday and Saturday, 6 a.m.–10:30 p.m.;
  Sunday, 7 a.m.–9:30 p.m.
  Bar hours: "open late"

Stuart Manor

7340 Garden Lane
Portage, MI 49024
(269) 329-5422
Website: portagemi.gov
Hours of operation: Monday–Friday 8 a.m.–5 p.m. Afternoon tea is held on
  the weekends. Please call for schedule and more information.

Upper Peninsula

Seul Choix Point Lighthouse
672N West Gulliver Lake Road
Gulliver, MI 49840
(906) 283-3860 May–September; (906) 283-3317 October–April
Website: greatlakelighthouse.com
Hours of operation: Open seven days a week, 10 a.m.–6 p.m.
Like most lighthouses, Seul Choix is only open from Memorial Day through
  mid-October.

Landmark Inn
230 North Front Street
Marquette, MI 49855
(906) 228-2580
Website: thelandmarkinn.com
There are three food venues on the property open throughout the day.

Calumet Theatre
340 Sixth Street
Calumet, MI 49913
(906) 337-2610
Website: calumettheatre.com
Hours of operation: The box office is open Wednesday–Friday, noon–
  5 p.m. and prior to performances.
Guided tours are available Monday–Friday, 11 a.m.–2 p.m. during the
  summer season only. Self-guided tours are permitted during box-office
  hours, but visitors should call ahead to make an appointment.

Whitefish Point Lighthouse and Shipwreck Museum
18335 N. Whitefish Point Road
Paradise, MI 49768
(888) 429-3747
Website: shipwreckmuseum.com
Hours of operation: The museum and lighthouse are open daily
  May 1–November 1.
Overnight accommodations are available in the Crew Quarters
  April 1–November 14.

Northern Michigan

Mission Table at Bowers Harbor Inn
13512 Peninsula Drive
Traverse City, MI 49686
(231) 223-4222
Website: missiontable.net
Hours of operation: Open only for dinner during the summer season and
for selected winter holidays. Check the website or call ahead to confirm.

Blue Pelican Inn
2535 North Main Street
Central Lake, MI 49622
(231) 544-2583
Website: thebluepelican.com
Hours of operation: The restaurant is open year-round, but the hours vary
according to the season.

Noggin Room and Stafford's Perry Hotel
100 Lewis Street
Petoskey, MI 49770
(231) 347-4000
Website for the Stafford's Perry Hotel: staffords.com/perry-hotel-4
Website for the Noggin Room Pub: staffords.com/noggin
Noggin Room's hours of operation:
    Sunday, noon–9 p.m. (bar stays open until 11 p.m.)
    Monday–Thursday, 4–9 p.m. (bar stays open until 11 p.m.)
    Friday, 4–10 p.m. (bar stays open until midnight)
    Saturday, 11:30 a.m.–10 p.m. (bar stays open until midnight)

City Park Grill
432 E. Lake Street
Petoskey, MI 49770
(231) 347-0101
Website: cityparkgrill.com
Hours of operation: Sunday–Thursday, 11:30 a.m.–9 p.m.;
    Friday and Saturday, 11:30 a.m.–10 p.m.

More Haunted Places to Visit

Cadieux Café, 4300 Cadieux Road, Detroit MI 48224, (313) 882-8560

Scarab Club, 217 Farnsworth Street, Detroit MI 48202, (313) 831-1250

Detroit Opera House, 1526 Broadway Street, Detroit MI 48226,
     (313) 237-7464

Bonstelle Theatre, 3424 Woodward Avenue, Detroit MI 48201,
     (313) 577-2960

Fort Wayne, 6325 West Jefferson Avenue, Detroit MI 48209, (313) 628-0796

Birmingham Theater, 211 South Woodward Avenue, Birmingham MI
     48009, (248) 644-3456

Albert's on the Alley, 5651 Middlebelt Road, Garden City MI 48135,
     (734) 525-5231

Lakeville Inn, 1318 Rochester Road, Leonard MI 48367, (248) 628-4460

Capitol Theatre, 140 E 2nd Street, Flint MI 48502, (810) 767-5141

Greenfield Village and Henry Ford Museum, 20900 Oakwood Boulevard,
     Dearborn, MI 48124, (313) 982-6001

Fox and Hound, 39560 Woodward Avenue, Bloomfield Hills MI 48304,
     (248) 644-4800

Midland Cinema, 6540 Cinema Drive, Midland MI 48642, (989) 839-0100

Murray Hotel, 7260 Main Street, Mackinac Island MI 49757, (855) 696-8772

Grand Hotel, 286 Grand Avenue, Mackinac Island MI 49757, (800) 334-7263

Island House Hotel, 6966 Main Street, Mackinac Island MI 49757, (906) 847-3347

Ste. Anne's Catholic Church, 6836 Main Street, Mackinac Island, MI 49757, (906) 847-3507

Cloghaun Bed-and-Breakfast, P.O. Box 1540, Mackinac Island MI 49757, (888) 442 5929

Crimson and Clover Floral and Gifts, 68085 South Main Street, Richmond MI 48062, (586) 727-0963

White Horse Inn, 1 East High Street, Metamora MI 48455, (810) 678-2150

Legendz Bar, 1631 Garfield St, Port Huron MI 48060, (810) 987-0856

Stafford's Weathervane Restaurant, 106 Pine River Lane, Charlevoix MI 49720, (231) 547-4311

Big Bay Lighthouse Bed-and-Breakfast, 4674 County Road Kcb, Big Bay MI 49808, (906) 345-9957

Old Presque Isle Lighthouse, 4500 E. Grand Lake Road, Presque Isle MI, on Lake Huron, (989)595-9917

Fairchild Theatre Auditorium (inside the Wharton Center), Michigan State University, East Lansing MI, (517) 432-2000

Tawas Point Lighthouse, Baldwin MI, (989) 362-5658

Grosvenor House Museum, 211 Maumee, St. Jonesville MI 49250-1246, (517)-849-9596

Bond Street Mansion, Niles MI 49120 (the house and crypt are private land, but it is believed that the ghostly aspirations of the former owners cross the street between the home and graveyard on a nightly basis).

River Raisin National Battlefield, 1403 East Elm Avenue, Monroe MI 48162, (734) 243-7136

Nunica Bar, 17040 112th Avenue, Nunica MI 49448, (616) 837-9752

Blackhawk Bar and Grill, 8940 North 32nd Street, Richland MI, 49083, (269) 629-9460

Wooden Nickel Saloon and Café, 1380 E Mason Street, Dansville MI, (517) 623-6589

Purple Rose Theatre, 137 Park Street, Chelsea MI 48118, (734) 433-7782

Howell Opera House, 123 West Grand River Avenue, Howell MI 48843, (517) 540-0065

Oak Hill Cemetery Battle Creek, home of the weeping statue known as "Crying Mary"

Sue's Lakeside Inn, 11303 East Chicago Road, Somerset MI 49281

Griswold Auditorium, 401 Hubbard St., Allegan MI 49010, (269) 673-3456

The Civic Theatre, 329 S. Park St., Kalamazoo MI 49007, (269) 343-0532

Georgie's Consignment Shop, 7504 Thornapple River Dr. SE, Ada MI 49301, (616) 676-1869

Old Jail Museum, 113 Walnut St., Allegan MI 49010, (269) 673-8292

Allegan Elks Lodge, 701 Marshall St., Allegan MI 49010, (269) 673-5656

Air Zoo, 6151 Portage Rd., Portage MI 49002, (269) 382-6555

Forest Roberts Theatre, 1401 Presque Isle Ave., Marquette Township MI 49855, (906) 227-2082

Antlers Restaurant, 804 East Portage Avenue, Sault Ste. Marie MI 49783, (906) 253-1728. Site of the 1913 Italian Hall Disaster in Calumet. There is a large historic marker in the park on the corner of Elm and 7th street, which is where the Italian Hall once stood.

Point Iroquois Lighthouse, open May 15 through October 15, 12942 West Lakeshore Drive, Brimley MI 49715, (906) 437-5272

Cadillac House, 5502 Main Street, Lexington, MI 48450 (810) 359-7201

House of Ludington, 223 Ludington Street, Escanaba MI 49829, (906) 786-6300

Big Rapids Cinema, 213 South Michigan Avenue, Big Rapids MI 49307, (231) 796-1452

Beckwith Theatre, 100 New York Avenue, Dowagiac MI 49047, (269) 782-7653

Ramsdell Theatre, 101 Maple Street, Manistee MI 49660, (231) 398-9770